Ken Davis is one of the best youth communicators anywhere, and his book *How to Speak to Youth* is the best on equipping my students to speak to youth! When I am responsible to help someone become a better communicator, whether one of my students or a mentoree, the first recommendation I always make is Ken Davis's *How to Speak to Youth*. It is the best resource for anyone who wants to be effective in communicating to today's young people.

Michael Holt, Professor of Youth Ministry, Columbia International University

If you read and apply the principles in *How to Speak to Youth and Keep Them Awake at the Same Time* your ability to communicate clearly and effectively will improve immediately. More importantly, Ken Davis will help you understand the Gospel, which deserves our best efforts! In his writing, Ken models and teaches effective communication through practical principles, personal stories, and insightful illustrations.

Lynn Ziegenfuss, Youth for Christ USA

Ken Davis presents timeless truths in a timely manner. This book is not a book for preachers about preaching. It's an exciting volume about communication for communicators. When speaking becomes exciting to the speaker, the hearers won't be far behind.

Fred W. Prinzing, Professor of Preaching and
Pastoral Ministry of Bethel Seminary

Ken is not just another speaker or writer ... He knows the art of communicating. I've seen him win the toughest audiences, in the most difficult situations. This book is prime example of his skill. It is brilliantly clear and practical. I haven't seen a better tool for learning and honing my communication abilities.

Lanny Donoho, President, Youth Ministry Resources, Atlanta, Georgia

This is the best book on how to speak to youth in the world. Ken Davis is my favorite communicator and the best at teaching others the trade.

Jim Burns, President, National Institute of Youth Ministry

Some people are so naturally gifted at what they do that they can't explain how to do it in terms the rest of us understand. Ken Davis offers us a rare opportunity to hear from a recognized master at speaking to teenagers who communicates his know-how with practical, down-to-earth principles that you can take to youth group next week! How he does all of that and still makes a book so doggone fun to read is a greater gift still. Get ready to learn a lot and laugh a lot. Even the most experienced communicator will pick up something helpful here.

Duffy Robbins, Dept. of Youth Ministry
Eastern College, St. Davids, Pennsylvania

Youth speakers and workers often operate at two extremes. They either entertain without purpose or they bore kids with important truth. In this book, Ken Davis combines over thirty years of practical experience with young people with critically important principles of communication. These insights and principles together maximize the potential for engaging AND meaningful messages. This unique combination makes this book a "must read" for anyone interested in effectively communicating to young people today.

Candie Blankman, Pastor, Educator, Speaker
Drew Blankman, Educator, Theologian, CBD Product Specialist

Ken Davis is more than a dynamic communicator, he is a dynamic teacher of communicators. His ability to dissect the speaking process and make it into easily understandable, usable, and practical principles is brilliant. But there is more to this book than just principles. Ken Davis is careful to emphasize the importance of the message and the messenger. Speaking, Ken says, is not only about a well-organized talk, it is about the integrity of the speaker. Ken's years of experience, his integrity, and his sense of humor combine to make this book a must for the professional and the nonprofessional alike.

Mike Yaconelli, Youth Specialties, North

I know from experience that when Ken Davis speaks, teenagers listen. Consequently, this is not only a must read book—this is a must re-read book for anybody interested in sharpening their communication skills. Thank you Ken, for sharing your insights and secrets with the rest of us.

Andy Stanley, North Park Community Church

How to Speak to Youth and Keep Them Awake at the Same Time strikes great balance between structure and content of a message, and presentation of that message. Ken's SCORRE model has changed how I prepare my own messages as well as how I teach others. It gives any speaker a workable structure to create messages that communicate with focus and clarity. Beyond just the mechanics of message construction, this book helps the speaker address style and presentation to maximize their ability to communicate with their audience. Ken's years of experience in speaking to young people, his insights into the uniqueness of an adolescent audience, and his passion to see anyone who gets in front of teenagers to present the Gospel with excellence makes this must reading for anyone in youth ministry!

While written in the framework of speaking to youth, the principles apply to speaking to audiences of any age. Whether you are new to public speaking and need a reference book on the basics of becoming an effective communicator, or a veteran speaker who is looking to refine and sharpen your presentations, I recommend How to Speak to Youth and Keep Them Awake at the Same Time. If every speaker could only have one book on the subject, this is it!

Gordy Smith, Area Director, Young Life, Chicago
Instructor, Evangelistic Communication to Youth,
Trinity Evangelical Divinity School, Deerfield, Illinois

In this book, Ken Davis clearly details the steps to becoming an effective communicator in any setting! As one of the country's best speakers, Ken's pragmatic approach to speaking will enable you to capture the hearts and minds of the young people you want to reach. Ken's use of modern communication theory coupled with many practical illustrations make this a must read for anyone called to speak to kids. I wholeheartedly recommend this fine book. (P.S. I even laughed out loud reading it!)

Chap Clark, Ph.D., Human Communication Studies Chair,
Youth and Family Ministry Department, Denver Seminary

REVISED EDITION

How to Speak to Youth...

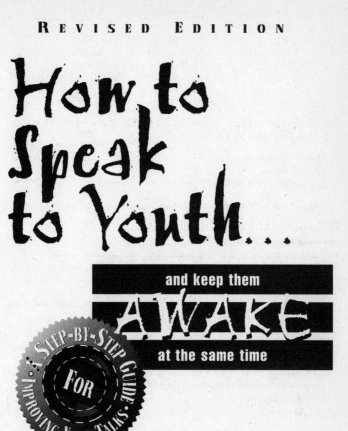

and keep them

AWAKE

at the same time

A STEP-BY-STEP GUIDE FOR IMPROVING YOUR TALKS

Ken Davis

ZondervanPublishingHouse

Grand Rapids, Michigan

A Division of HarperCollinsPublishers

How to Speak to Youth ... and Keep Them Awake at the Same Time
Copyright © 1986 by Ken Davis

How to Speak to Youth ... and Keep Them Awake at the Same Time
Revised edition
Copyright © 1996 by Ken Davis

Requests for information should be addressed to:

⚓ ZondervanPublishingHouse
Grand Rapids, Michigan 49530

Library of Congress Cataloging-in-Publication Data

Davis, Ken, 1946–
    How to speak to youth—and keep them awake at the same time : a step-by-step guide for improving your talks / Ken Davis.
        p. cm.
    Originally published: Loveland, Colo. : Group Books, 1986.
    ISBN: 0-310-20146-2 (softcover)
    1. Church group work with youth. 2. Preaching to youth. 3.
Communication—Religious aspects—Christianity. I. Title.
BV4447.D38 1996
259'.23—dc 20   96-22545
        CIP

Revised edition edited by Mary McNeil
Interior design by Sue Koppenol
Illustrated by Rand Kruback

Printed in the United States of America

---

97 98 99 00 01 02 03 / ❖ DH/ 10 9 8 7 6 5 4 3

To these people whose personal dedication
to youth changed my life forever:
Francis Peterson, Bud Hanke, Gary Werner,
Harold Andrews, Robert Thompson, Bob Tanner,
and Ned Brande

CONTENTS

PART TWO
PRESENTATION: ONCE YOUR LIPS START MOVING

PART THREE
PROGRESS: ADVANCED LIP MOVES

FOREWORD

I always knew Ken Davis was an entertaining speaker, but I didn't know the full extent of his gifts until I saw him "do his thing" a few years ago at a youth convention. I was a speaker at the same convention, and it was my task to provide the daily morning Bible studies. Following my presentations, the kids participated in discussion groups, special seminars, and all the other activities that typify such conventions. Each evening featured a special speaker who brought the day's activities to a climactic conclusion.

To say that the conference was not going well the first few days would be an understatement. The young people were exhausted, having traveled long distances to get to the conference. The huge meeting hall contained no chairs, which made it necessary for the participants to make themselves as comfortable as possible on the hardwood floors. The acoustics in the barnlike building were terrible, the sound system poor, and the atmosphere stifling. It seemed as though the convention was heading for disaster. But then Ken Davis arrived, and everything turned around.

Ken was the scheduled speaker for the Wednesday evening session. The young people greeted him with polite applause, and they offered him the same discourteous lack of interest they had offered the other speakers. But Ken seemed undisturbed by it all. He went ahead and gave his talk in an enthusiastic, committed manner. Within minutes he had the group's undivided attention. With each passing story and illustration, interest intensified. During the next fifty minutes he carried the kids through a whole range of emotions. He had them laughing and crying. He had them shouting and sitting in stark silence. He communicated a Christian message with profound content.

When Ken finished his talk, the crowd gave him a standing ovation. It had been more than the performance of a good entertainer; it had been a time in which a servant of God used his talents to lead hundreds of young people into thoughtful consideration of the Gospel.

Following Ken's presentation, the atmosphere at the convention changed. The next morning the young people greeted me with rapt attention. They hung on my every word. The song leaders found that the crowd enthusiastically followed them.

In one address, Ken Davis had done more than just entertain, he made the kids want to listen and respond. He set the stage for one of my most positive experiences in speaking to a group of young people. Many times while reflecting on that week, I have said to myself, "We need more speakers who can do for young people what Ken Davis did for those kids on that crucial evening."

There is only one Ken Davis, and I'm not suggesting that God should clone him. Furthermore, young, fledgling speakers would make a terrible mistake by trying to imitate his style, gestures, and mannerisms. Ken Davis is Ken Davis, and nobody else should try to be like him. However, we can learn from Ken Davis without imitating him. And I am happy that he wrote this book, so that all of us might do just that.

In *How to Speak to Youth . . . and Keep Them Awake at the Same Time*, Ken helps us realize that being a good speaker is ten percent inspiration and ninety percent perspiration. He gives ample evidence that even though he comes across as being spontaneous and "off the cuff," his messages are well contrived and carefully planned. Ken shows us that the brilliant stories that he uses to illustrate the major points of his talk are carefully constructed, repeatedly rehearsed, and prayerfully put together.

He makes it clear that being a good speaker does not come from seeking to entertain, but from seeking to communicate a great truth. Humor, which he constantly employs in his presentations, is a means to an end and never an end in itself. Ken shows us that behind his easygoing presentations of the Gospel, there has been care, planning, practice, and most of all, a dependence on God.

Poor preaching is responsible for a lot of poor presentations of the Gospel and the loss of a host of opportunities to lead people into the kingdom of God. I am in no way minimizing relational ministries when I extol the importance of good preaching. We need effective, relational ministries, but we also need persons who know how to craft good messages that will communicate the Gospel with clarity and effectiveness.

If you are interested in the procedure of preparing a good talk, if you are trying to figure out the most effective ways to communicate the Gospel to young people, and if you are anxious to speak in a manner that leads kids to make decisions about their commitment to Christ, you will find this book of immeasurable help.

Anthony Campolo

WHY THIS BOOK WAS WRITTEN (AND REWRITTEN)

The requests started coming in over twenty years ago. Youth leaders, laypeople, pastors, and even teenagers asked, "How did you learn to communicate so well? How can I learn to do the same?" At first the questions embarrassed me—partly because I was unwilling to accept the fact that my speaking was any good, and partly because I didn't know what made the difference between a good and a bad speech. When corporations began to pay large sums of money to have me speak to their employees, and when the phone started ringing with more requests than I possibly could handle, I began to believe that I must be doing something right (although I still had no idea what that "right thing" was). By this time, the letters and phone calls asking for help in developing speaking skills had reached a significant number. I decided it was time to research and identify some of the elements of good communication.

There are three truths about good communication that inspired the writing and rewriting of this book.

Truth #1: Excellent communication skills come only as a result of very hard work. Young men and women often call seeking some secret to suddenly becoming a good communicator. They are seldom pleased with my response. No single learning experience can transform a person into an overnight speaking sensation.

Although some find it easier than others, no one is born with the gift of being an excellent communicator. Communication skills must be developed through education and experience. That process takes time. Several years ago when I was asked why I was able to hold the attention of an audience, I could not come up with a specific answer. I thought it was simply a gift. I neglected the fact I had accumulated years of experience working with high school students in the Youth for Christ program. I took for granted the thousands of speeches I had given to a wide variety of audiences. I neglected the influence of speaking to over one million students in high school assemblies. Every one of those speeches was a learning experience, a training ground. It wasn't until I had given thousands of talks that people began to notice "special skills."

Once I had compiled the information for this book, I also realized there was much room for improvement in my own presentations. I spent years developing only the entertainment aspect of my speaking. Effective communication goes so much further than just being interesting. Roadkill is interesting, but it rarely affects the quality of your life. I needed to focus my efforts to maximize the message I had been entrusted with. Even today I am continually striving to improve. Effective communication is an endeavor so challenging that the work is never done. There is always room for improvement.

Truth #2: Good communication can be learned. As we developed the Dynamic Communicators Workshop, I watched hundreds of students improve their communication skills in a relatively short period of time. Information that had taken me years of experience to learn could be taught in just a few days and put to use immediately. The information is of value if you remember that good communication goes beyond theory. You must reach further than just the memorization of the principles that make a good communicator. Many people with graduate degrees in communication can't communicate their way out of a wet paper bag.

Conversely, I have met men and women without formal training who outshine many of their educated peers. It is the combination of knowledge, application, and experience that makes the difference.

Truth #3: There is a missing element in most speech communication courses. This missing element involves learning to communicate with "heart." Imagine yourself listening to two pianists of equal ability playing the same piece. One's playing is technically correct, while the other plays with feeling and heart. How do you respond? Without a doubt you find the second piece much more enjoyable. In one you hear correct notes, in the other you are moved by those notes.

There are some aspects about communicating with heart that cannot be taught. They spring naturally from the character and passion of the speaker. But there are ways to develop that character and tap into that passion. Learning how to be vulnerable, knowing how to establish rapport, and developing a sensitivity to the audience are all skills that can move speeches from sounding canned and mechanical to being dynamic and powerful.

This book covers the entire spectrum of skills that lead to powerful communication. If excellent communication skills come as a result of hard work, then it follows that this book can't do all the hard work for you. However, the fact that you are reading this book would indicate that you are willing to put forth some effort to develop your speaking skills. The commitment to practice and the willingness to pay the price of excellence are yours to invest. By passing on what God has allowed me to learn through hours of research and thirty years of experience, I can save you some time and effort.

Watching the progress of thousands of people who have attended our Dynamic Communicators Workshops has proven that these principles work. They can transform your ministry if you choose to apply them.

So, why did I do a second edition? The ten years of experience since *How to Speak to Youth* was first written have taught me many new lessons. I rewrote this book for three reasons.

First, there has been a significant change in our culture. Although our message never changes, the method of communicating that message must keep up with the culture. Before missionaries set foot on foreign soil they spend months studying the customs, language, and traditions of the culture to ensure that they can effectively communicate the Gospel. If you work with youth, you are a missionary. You too must learn the language and customs of a strange and ever-changing culture. Some aspects of the youth culture change in a matter of weeks, so you can imagine how many changes have taken place in ten years. Ten years ago "rap" was something you did to a sandwich to keep it fresh. Twenty years ago, personal video was still a novelty and personal computers were only for the rich. Access to the Internet wasn't available to the general public. Telly Savalas was famous for his shaved head, but no student would have gone to school with his head shaved or his initials shaved into his scalp. Today, heads read like bulletin boards. It's time I brought this up to date.

Second, experience has taught me that some of my earlier thinking was faulty and in some cases flat-out wrong. You will find many places in this edition where I have taken the opportunity to correct those misconceptions.

Last, I have changed. As I read again the thoughts that I penned the first time around, I was pleased that I still felt passionate about most of them. The basic principles are still viable and necessary for excellence in communication. But I was surprised at how my perspective had changed. I still believe in those principles, but now I present them from what I hope is a more mature and helpful perspective.

You will find this book useful, enjoyable, and easy to read. I hope you will discipline yourself to apply what you learn to your communication with youth. Your audience deserves, and sometimes demands, the very best. As messengers of the King, we can't afford to settle for anything less.

PART ONE
PREPARATION:

Before You Move Your Lips

CHAPTER ONE

Personal Preparation

Before we ever open our mouths or put a pencil to a piece of paper, our communication potential will be affected by these aspects of our life: our dedication to the importance of the message, our understanding and commitment to our audience, our confidence that we will be heard, and our own personal growth.

THE MESSAGE: WHY SAY ANYTHING AT ALL?

Of all the communicators in the world, none have a more important message or more potential for a dynamic and powerful delivery than those who are messengers of the Gospel of Jesus Christ. Both the message and the youthful audience to whom we have been called to deliver that message account for the potential. The most effective communicators are always those with an important cause in which they believe intensely.

I remember selling home-study courses shortly after I got out of college. Like many college graduates, I was starving and desperately in need of money. There was a $150 commission on the sale of each course. At the time, $150 was a small fortune. Although the product was not very good and did little to help the customer, the money was more than I could resist. It took seven days for me to perfect what I thought was the most dynamic sales presentation ever devised. The presentation was so good, I was tempted to buy a study course for myself. The day my presentation was perfected, I sold the first course. The next day I sold two. My prospects were so eager to buy, I couldn't believe it. After selling five courses and feeling flush with $750 stretching my pockets, I decided it was time to try to sell one outside the family. I had run out of relatives. After just two days of turndowns and slammed doors, I quit. Had I been selling a product I believed in and felt would really help my customers, I might have had the motivation to weather those rough times. But money was my only motive. At the first sign of resistance, I gave up.

Howard Hendricks once said, "If a person goes into youth work for the money, they probably don't have the intelligence for the job." So money is probably not a motivating factor. In fact, there will be many rough times in every youth worker's experience. Youth work is neither glamorous nor frivolous. It is hard work and has many discouraging moments. No speaking course, book, or paycheck will take us through those tough times. Sharing the message of Christ's love with the young people of our world is a challenge unequaled in its importance and urgency. Only an unquenchable desire to share that message of love will carry us through.

THE AUDIENCE: WHO'S LISTENING?

We can approach our ministry with such a sense of commitment because we have the opportunity to address the most challenging, unique, and wonderful audience in the world. On the one hand, young people are hostile and skeptical, spoiled by a barrage of top-quality entertainment and turned off to much of traditional religion. On the other hand, they are moldable and tender, capable of great loyalty and commitment. Our audience is a self-conscious group of teenagers, who spend much of their lives wondering what their friends will think and giving very little thought to their own goals. They grow up in a culture that teaches them to avoid sacrifice and pain. Many kids live only for themselves and for immediate gratification.

They want to believe they will live forever, yet they fear death and try to cram all of life into today. Many teenagers are lonely even in the midst of a crowd of their peers. They want to be noticed but are afraid to be different unless there is a group willing to be different with them. Many of their role models present a message that is the antithesis of the Gospel.

The previously mentioned characteristics are constantly changing. The postwar '50s spawned a group of young people who were extremely aware that World War II had been ended by a weapon that also was capable of ending the world. This was my generation, and I remember well the "eat, drink, and be merry, for tomorrow you may die" mind-set.

The '60s delivered a generation that was actively involved in politics and moral issues. Many children of that

period rejected their parents' materialism and dropped out of society. They were known as the antiestablishment generation. They were cause-oriented and were willing to commit themselves to those causes, even at great sacrifice. During that period, many young men went to jail as a result of their opposition to a confusing and demoralizing war. On the flip side, intense dedication led thousands of young men to fight and lose their lives in that same war.

The '70s saw much of that same generation demoralized and defeated. The great changes they had hoped to achieve didn't materialize. Many of the revolutionary leaders of that day were absorbed into the very system they previously had fought. So the late '70s and early '80s brought us full circle to a materialistic generation of young people for whom the weekend party was about as far ahead as they wished to think. The rebellious and dangerous use of experimental drugs diminished to a more predictable dependence on alcohol and pot for a high. Materialism was "in" once again. The old, beat-up psychedelic vans were replaced by BMWs; the hippies were replaced by the yuppies.

The generation of the '90s is populated by a culture of teenagers who are disillusioned and demoralized (in the truest sense of the word). They bought into the philosophy that says there are no absolutes. With no distinction between right and wrong, they celebrate a freedom that is really no freedom at all. In many ways they are in bondage. Either they are frozen in fear because they lack the moral boundaries to guide them, or they are prisoners to the consequences of living without those boundaries. They have grown up seeing less of their parents and more of the evil in the world than any previous generation. They watch the world in fast-forward. The Gulf War, the L.A. riots, the O. J. trial, the Oklahoma City bombing all flash past faster than teenagers can process them. They are without heroes. They are desperate for love, in need of guidelines, and seeking a reason to live. In a relativistic world, they don't know where to turn. If ever there was a lost generation, this is it.

Keeping up with the changes in our youth culture is not an easy task. We must be careful not to fall into the trap of believing that the methods that worked last year still will be effective this year. One way to keep up is by reading. It is imperative that communicators who wish to relate to the current youth culture keep current themselves. Trends in teenagers' attitudes and behaviors can be gleaned from news magazines, psychology magazines, magazines the teenagers themselves read, and studies on trends in the youth culture.

We also can keep current by listening. Music always has been a reflection of the views and attitudes of a culture. Although we may not agree with the attitudes, direction, or style of the music kids enjoy, it would serve us well to listen. Listening to the music kids like helps us understand their thinking and their behavior. Keep current by finding out what television programs are favorites among teenagers. Ask yourself, "What needs are being met by this programming?" Some of these popular programs are not what one would call "quality" television. Then what is it that makes kids watch?

Most important in keeping up with the changes in any culture is to immerse ourselves in the people of that culture. We could read every study ever published on youth, watch every form of entertainment available to teenagers, listen to every album that ever hit the charts, and still miss the mark in understanding our kids. When missionaries wish to understand a new and strange culture (the youth culture is always new and strange), they go to live with the people of that culture. We will be able to identify with the needs of teenagers only if we see them where they live—if we see their homes, attend their games, chaperone their dances, attend their plays, listen to their humor, and so forth. If we live where they live, we will not be left behind. The day we become only a facilitator of programming or a researcher of youth behavior, we will lose touch and our audience will change. If we don't adapt to that change, our message will not be heard. We will become old-fashioned speakers, hired and enjoyed by old-fashioned people, but alienated from a new generation. The life-changing message of Christ's love and forgiveness will never change, but our methods of delivering that message must be updated constantly.

This generation of teenagers has more material advantages than any generation in history. They have access to the best entertainment Hollywood can offer. Although we need to make every effort to ensure that our programs are entertaining and interesting, sooner or later we must come to the realization that we cannot compete with the material resources or the high-tech images of Hollywood. But there is hope. Close observation reveals that television, movies, high-tech games, and possessions are not giving our kids what they need most. In spite of all these "advantages," our children are taking their own lives at an alarming rate. Every year close to 500,000 teenagers attempt to kill themselves. Countless others live only for the moment, making decisions that rob their lives of future potential. Others simply stumble through life in a quiet, hopeless despair, hiding from real life by immersing themselves in a world of fantasy, parties, and entertainment.

None of these advantages touch the deep needs that tug at their hearts. They are starved for a sense of self-worth and have a desperate need to be involved. They need to know that someone cares, and they need to be called to a deeper relationship with a God who loves them. What a challenge! We stand in the gap. We offer a message of hope. We can provide a community of love and caring that no video or movie can give. What Christ has to offer meets those deepest needs. But today's teenagers are receiving conflicting messages from every quarter. Our voice is just one among many screaming for their attention. Why should they listen to us?

THE METHOD: HOW WILL THEY HEAR MY VOICE?

In the midst of tough competition from all quarters, how do we reach the kids? Jim Green, a veteran of youth ministry, encouraged me to try a group experience that illustrated how we can make our voice heard amidst the din. We conducted a three-phase experiment at Rockford College, using over one hundred college graduates who were preparing for youth ministry.

In the first phase, we took a young volunteer from the room and blindfolded him. We simply told him that when he returned, he could do anything he wished. He remained outside the room while we instructed each audience member to think of a simple task for the volunteer to do (a task the volunteer could complete inside the lecture hall). When the volunteer returned, they were to shout their individual instructions at him from where they sat. Prior to this, we privately instructed a second volunteer. As though it were a matter of life and death, this person was to attempt to persuade the blindfolded volunteer to climb the steps at the back of the auditorium and embrace an instructor who was standing at the door. The catch was that he had to shout this vital message from where he sat in the audience. The original volunteer was unaware of all instructions and previous arrangements.

The volunteer represented our young people, the audience represented the world of voices screaming for their attention, and the person with the vital message represented those of us who bring the message of the Gospel to youth.

The first phase was now set, and the blindfolded student was led back into the room. The lecture room exploded in a din of shouting. Each person tried to get the volunteer to follow his or her unique instructions. In the midst of the crowd, the voice of the person with the vital message was lost; no single message stood out. The blindfolded student stood paralyzed by confusion and indecision. He moved randomly and without purpose as he sought to discern a clear and unmistakable voice in the crowd. After a few minutes the first phase ended. We sent the volunteer from the room and compared the experience to our situation as youth communicators. Our vital message, eloquent as it might be, often is lost amid the barrage of other voices constantly shouting conflicting and confusing messages to our young people.

After a brief discussion, we explained the second phase of our experiment. We told the audience about the person attempting to get the volunteer to accomplish the vital task. At this point, we chose another person from the audience to add a new dimension. This person's goal was to, at all costs, keep the volunteer from doing the vital task. While the rest of the audience was to remain in their seats, these two people were allowed to stand next to the volunteer and shout their opposing messages. They could get as close as they wished; however, they were not allowed to touch the volunteer. As the blindfolded volunteer was led back into the room, the shouting began again. I couldn't hear myself think! This time, because the two messengers were standing so close, the volunteer could hear both messages; but because the messages were opposed to each other, he vacillated. He followed one for a bit, then was convinced by the other to go in the opposite direction. After a few minutes of this seesaw behavior, we stopped the second phase and again led the volunteer from the room. As a group we discussed this uncanny parallel to our own situations: In order for young people to hear our message we must get close to them. Even then, there are others with opposing messages who also are close enough to make their messages clear. Sometimes they are peers, other times they are relatives, and sometimes they are those who simply vie for our teenagers' dollars and don't even care about them as people. Very often our young people respond just as the volunteer did. One day they are committed, the next day they give in to the pressures of other voices. The main lesson in the second phase was that only the close voices could be heard. Even though the volunteer took no decisive action, at last he heard the message.

The response to the third phase was startling. In this phase everything remained the same except the one with the vital message was allowed to touch the volunteer. He could not pull, push, or in any way force the volunteer to do his bidding; but he could touch him, and in that way encourage him to follow. The blindfolded volunteer was led into the room. When he appeared, the silence erupted into an earsplitting roar. The two messengers stood close, shouting their opposing words.

Then the one with the vital message put his arm gently around the volunteer's shoulder and leaned very close to speak directly into his ear. Almost without hesitation, the volunteer began to yield to his instruction. Occasionally he paused to listen as the opposition frantically tried to convince him to turn around. But then because of the gentle touch of the one with the vital message, he allowed himself to be guided on. A moment of frightening realism occurred spontaneously as the one with the vital message grew close to the goal. All those in the audience, who, up to this point, had been shouting their own individual instruction, suddenly joined in unison to keep the volunteer from taking those final steps.

Goose bumps appeared all over my body as students began to chant together, "Don't go!" "Don't go!" "Don't go!" So many times I've seen the forces that pull our youth in different directions join together to dissuade them from a serious commitment to Christ. The chant grew to a pulsing crescendo, "Don't go!" "Don't go!" But the guiding arm of the one with the vital message never left the volunteer's shoulder. At the top of the stairs in the back of the lecture hall, the one with the vital message leaned one last time to whisper in the ear of the volunteer. There was a moment of hesitation, then the volunteer threw his arms around the instructor and the auditorium erupted in cheers and applause. There were more than a few damp eyes in the room as many of us were touched with the truth of what we had just seen.

When the volunteer revealed how he felt as he went through each phase, it became apparent that if our message is to be heard, we cannot shout it from the cavernous confines of our church buildings. We must venture out and draw close to those with whom we wish to communicate. If we really seek a life-changing commitment from our young people, we also much reach out where they are and, in love, gently touch them and lead them to that commitment. We asked the volunteer why he followed the one with the vital message, the one who

touched him. After a few moments he said, "Because it felt like he was the only one who really cared."

Years ago I became fascinated with memory. Probably because I never had one. I learned a technique that would enable me to memorize the names of over 300 people, having met them just one time. Armed with this secret I headed out to speak at a youth camp in Florida. As the kids came into the dining hall that first evening I greeted each of them at the door and asked their name. Using my new system I memorized the names of over two hundred campers. I only needed review on three or four. All week long, whenever I would see a camper, I would greet that person by name. I looked at the whole experience as an interesting demonstration of a memory technique and a way to impress kids. But the campers saw it much differently. I never saw a more effective week of ministry. The response of those teenagers to the Gospel and their openness to me remains unprecedented. They believed that they were more to me than just campers, and I was more than just the speaker. I was a friend who knew their name. My voice was heard and the message accepted because I had touched them.

Every year I get hundreds of letters and phone calls from young men and women who want to minister to youth by traveling and speaking as I do. I am always careful to remind them that the front lines of youth ministry are not defined by a podium or stage. The most effective way to reach teenagers is to live among them, to hurt when they hurt, to be there to pick them up when they fall. The everyday contact that is available only to the youth worker defines the front lines of ministry. In a sea of conflicting voices, your ability to touch kids by loving them where they live will make your voice heard.

THE MESSENGER: LOOK WHO'S TALKING!

If we clearly understand the importance of our message, if we understand our audience, and if we know how to make our message heard, then we have to ask what we can do to prepare ourselves for this task. Following are four "essentials" for effective communication.

We Must Be Committed to Practicing What We Preach

Our lives are the greatest illustrations of the message most kids will see. Our lives are living testimony to the truth and power of our message and the very foundation of its effectiveness.

The most effective communicators I know—those who get results—are not necessarily the most eloquent, but instead are those who believe in their message enough to live it and deliver it with passion. I once sat under the ministry of a very eloquent and charismatic youth speaker. He was new to the church and well liked. He brought many new young people into the church. Unknown to us, his personal life was devoid of the joy and knowledge of the Christ he spoke about. His messages soon sounded hollow. As my friends and I discovered that his words were empty, we were no longer moved by his eloquence.

In contrast, I once was asked to train a couple from a small farming town to work with young people. They were a wonderful couple, but I didn't think they had the flash and slickness that at the time I felt was essential for effective youth ministry. (After all, you have to be cool to work with teenagers!) I don't think either of these people would have defined themselves as "cool," but they were real. They had a simple faith in Christ that was evidenced in their everyday lives. Their faith was accompanied by an insatiable love for the kids with whom they worked. The result was a ministry that outshined most of us "cool," city-slicker trainers. No one will ever pay these people great sums of money to come and speak, but I have met scores of teenagers who will be eternally indebted to them because they cared enough to minister. It was this couple's love and the example of their faith that did what all the training and eloquence in the world can't do. This couple practiced what they preached.

Shortly after I began to be active as a corporate speaker and motivator, I became aware of a large sales convention in our state. Several thousand salespeople attended this convention, and I desperately wanted a chance to speak to this group. I thought the past convention speakers were less than dynamic, and I knew I could do a much better job of motivating these people to even greater sales. When I approached the president, he was very excited about having me speak to his group; however, as a condition, I had to join the sales force. This required a commitment of time and money I was unwilling to make. I never was allowed to address this group. For a while I was very disappointed; however, after more thought I realized the president was right. How could I possibly motivate people to a commitment I was unwilling to make myself? We must practice what we preach.

We Must Be Committed to Being Ourselves

I remember meeting a young man who had just accepted a position as youth pastor for a large church. As we conversed, I was impressed with his intelligence and his genuine manner. I looked forward to hearing him speak that evening to a large group of teenagers. His program was interesting and varied, and I was impressed with how he took control of the meeting. When he picked up his Bible to deliver his talk, a strange metamorphosis took place. In front of my eyes this young pastor changed into "Billy Graham"—his mannerisms, the way he held his Bible, the tone and inflection of his voice, everything! The talent and control he had demonstrated earlier were gone. Near the beginning of his devotional, he began to lose his audience. They were polite, but it was obvious many were no longer listening. That look of genuine interest and rapport was gone from all but a few. Out of those who still were showing interest, I believe many were missing the message as they concentrated on the excellent impersonation of Billy Graham. My wife broke my thoughts as she leaned over to whisper her amazement at the great likeness. The message was good, but the content was lost. It was upstaged by a great Billy Graham impersonation.

This story is extreme, but it illustrates a point. Be yourself. You don't need to develop a weepy, shaky preaching voice. You don't need to furrow your brow and take on an air of authority. You need to be you. Trying to copy someone else's style or mannerisms only dilutes you. You are the messenger. Teenagers may be amused at your likeness to some great television preacher, but when it comes time to be touched by God's Word or when they need personal help and counsel, kids will want to communicate with someone who is genuine. Even when I was a child I was irritated by the trembling preaching and praying intonation of men who in real life could speak quite normally. I still speak to young people who say, "I don't know how to pray." They assume that to pray "correctly" one must know how to speak in a trembling voice, arrange the words in prehistoric sentence construction, and assume a "spiritual" tone. Many teenagers add this to a list of evidence that leads them to the wrong assumption that Christianity is not relevant for today.

People who try to be like someone else communicate that they are not pleased with themselves. Of course there will be times when you will assume the role of a character to illustrate a point. But overall, the person kids see when you are communicating God's Word should be the same person they see in everyday life. Use whatever techniques necessary to enhance your message, but be yourself. The most valuable paintings in the world are originals, not copies of originals.

It is also a mistake to feel you must act like a kid to win a hearing. We live in a world where many kids fear growing older. Much of their fear comes from seeing adults who are afraid to be adults. Instead they see frustrated adults trying to be kids. Have fun, get involved, but be yourself. Teenagers need to see an adult comfortable with being an adult. When young people seek an adult for help, they are not going to confide in someone who is immature. They will go to someone who has demonstrated adult wisdom and confidence. Some-

one who does not desperately seek their approval by acting like a teenager.

Some adults try to act like kids, while others try to dress like kids. Fashion is an element of communication that may seem insignificant to us, but it is important to today's socially conscious teenager. I asked my teenage sister, "What makes you listen to a speaker?"

Her response was, "If the guy comes out in a three-piece polyester leisure suit, I won't hear a word he says."

We need not wear a pair of baggy pants at half-mast or have our tongue pierced in order to communicate with teenagers who have adopted these styles. But by the same token we should put away our Tory wigs, polyester hand-me-downs, and knickers and at least be contemporary in our dress. We also need to be careful in our grooming. We communicate a lack of concern when we appear disheveled. If a speaker has long, dirty fingernails, people will focus only on those fingernails! Be an outgoing, fun-loving, adventurous adult. Model the fact that adults actually can have fun. Model the truth that life with Christ is worthwhile at any age.

In order to be yourself you must know who you are. Are you generally a happy-go-lucky, witty person who often cracks jokes and is the life of the party? (It's okay to answer yes.) Then that's you, and you're very special. That uniqueness will show through in everything you do. One of my good friends enjoys comedy and humor as much as I do. He is called often to speak in rather formal situations. He responds by being appropriately formal and serious and does very well, but the lightness of his heart beams from everywhere—from the twinkle in his eye to the wry humor of his illustrations. He teaches and preaches serious messages, but he does not pretend to be a serious person. He allows the real person to show through.

Conversely, one of the saddest (almost pitiful) speakers is the one who has no natural sense of humor but tries to be a comedian. It's okay to be serious. I just can't picture the apostle Paul saying, "Hey, guys, I heard a great one today. Two Jews walked into a bar . . ." Maybe Peter or Andrew could have done this, but not Paul. Although he may have had a sense of humor, it would have been expressed as part of his serious nature. He was so intense; however, I'd be willing to bet that when he did laugh, it was a great laugh. Later in this book, we discuss how it is possible to develop humor in your message using your own style and personality. Some of the greatest youth ministers I know are over fifty and are not especially funny people. They know how to use humor within the context of who they are. They don't try to be someone else.

So many times youth leaders, pastors, and others who are required to speak as a part of their vocation have said, "Ken, I wish I had your sense of humor. I would love to hold the attention of an audience as you do." It's ironic that I often have wished I had the skills of the great Bible teachers. At one time I wanted desperately to be known for my serious approach to the Scriptures. Even though I am a student of theology and clearly present biblical truth, I have come to realize I will never be thought of as a deep theological teacher. I know who I am. I am fully aware of the gifts I have been given. I will be as intense as ever in my quest to communicate solid biblical truth, but the real me always will show through. Be yourself.

We Must Be Committed to Glorifying God

One of the most beautiful gems in the world is a diamond. Its value stems from its brilliance. Every color of the rainbow can be seen in its sparkle. The reason for a diamond's beautiful brilliance is that it reflects almost all the light that comes to it. On the other hand, a plain old rock absorbs almost all light. It isn't often you find people standing around "oohing" and "aahing" over an ordinary rock.

A communicator can very easily absorb all the light. Effective communication is a very powerful tool. Holding an audience in the palm of your hand is an exhilarating and heady experience. It is easy to absorb attention and praise in the mistaken belief that it makes one more powerful and brilliant. In truth, our message is one of life and light. When we reflect audience adoration and praise back to Jesus Christ, while at the same time reflecting his love to our audience, we are lifted from the pettiness of egotism and shine with the brilliance of a diamond!

This contrast was observed with clarity at an event that featured several Christian music groups. These groups had received celebrity status in some Christian circles. When the event was over, the adoring crowd of teenagers rushed the stage for autographs. One young performer, by his actions and words, made it plain that he felt he was worthy of the kids' praise. He told them he was tired from the "gig" and could only grant a short time for autographs. This young man's ego was so outrageous he succeeded in turning off some of his own admirers. I heard one teenager comment, "I guess he's his own best fan."

On the opposite side of the stage was another group signing autographs. Rather than promoting the "aren't we great" attitude, they were using their popularity to minister to kids. One group member sat for fifteen minutes with a paraplegic teenager who had been wheeled up to get an autograph. Another group member sat cross-legged on the floor dealing with the spiritual struggles of a searching teenager. These performers were vulnerable and caring; the contrast between the two groups was obvious to many who attended. One was a "rock" group (a group of rocks). The other group was made up of diamonds. Reflect the light!

We Must Be Committed to Excellence

If we truly believe ours is the greatest message in the world, and if we are convinced that the young people to whom we minister need to hear that message, then we must strive for excellence at every step in the preparation and delivery of that message. If we are representatives of the King of kings and Lord of lords and are entrusted with proclaiming his redemptive love and grace, then mediocrity is not an option.

Although we strive for excellence it is important to remember God's role in all this. Youth work is more of a calling than it is a profession. Even though we are responsible for being the best we can be, it is God's blessing that brings fruit from our ministry. Moses stuttered and spoke poorly; Paul admitted he was not eloquent. In fact, Paul was so boring his speaking once killed a man. Remember Eutychus, the young man who fell asleep listening to Paul speak? He fell from a window and died. Eutychus was "sinking into a deep sleep as Paul talked on and on. When he was sound asleep, he fell to the ground from the third story and was picked up dead" (Acts 20:9). Now that is boring! But God bypassed eloquent speakers and chose Moses (instead of silver-tongued Aaron) to lead his people from bondage, and he chose Paul to be one of the greatest apostles.

I am always amazed on those nights when I feel I have blundered through the evening with snowmobile boots in my mouth, and God chooses those very evenings to do his greatest work. In 1991 I had the privilege of speaking to 11,000 teenagers gathered in Washington, D.C., for Youth for Christ's "DC 91" event. I struggled that night as never before. My humor seemed to fall flat and I couldn't seem to make clear the message I had so carefully prepared. Sweating profusely, I closed the service with what I felt was a weak call to commitment. I left the stage in tears, privately making a vow never to accept such a responsibility again. Backstage I met Roger Cross, the president of Youth for Christ. I embraced him, blubbered my apology for such a poor performance, and asked for his forgiveness. With tears in his own eyes, Roger led me back to the edge of that massive stage. "Look," he said, forcing me to look out over that huge convention center. Teenagers were streaming from everywhere, making their way to the front of the building to proclaim their commitment to a living Christ. That night many hundreds responded to the urging of the Holy Spirit through the message I had delivered. Perhaps one of the steps to success as a communicator is to never forget:

We are privileged to be the best we can be at any given moment, but ultimately, it is God's work.

I assume that the reason you purchased this book (besides your good taste in authors) is that you want to strive for excellence in the proclamation of God's Word. In that endeavor, we are of kindred heart. Over the past thirty years, God has blessed me with a fruitful ministry to millions of youth and adults. Through our Dynamic Communicators Workshops, I also have been privileged to observe and train thousands of youth workers from around the world. I want to pass on to you whatever insight and knowledge has come from my experience, so that together we might continue in excellence toward our common goal of bringing the transforming power of Christ's love to the receptive hearts of young people everywhere.

CHAPTER TWO

Objective Preparation

Mastering the basics is essential to experiencing the best. Vince Lombardi is considered by many to be one of the most effective coaches of all time. Whenever the Green Bay Packers began to falter from their usual championship-style performance, Lombardi always responded by going back to the basics. There was nothing glamorous about practicing the basic technique of running a play until perfect, yet the Packers' championship style was built on that basic technique. This chapter will discuss a proven basic technique that can serve as a foundation for championship communication.

THE SCORRE METHOD: IF YOU DON'T KNOW WHAT YOU'RE AIMING AT, YOU'LL NEVER HIT IT

When I was a teenager, deer hunting was the method we used to provide meat for our family in the winter. One cold, crisp fall morning, while hunting a tract of land near our home, I heard a shot ring out. The bullet hit a tree next to my face. My mind made a mental note of how close that must have been and I continued walking. A second shot clipped through the branches just over my head. I winced and again thought of what a coincidence it was that there should be two shots that would come so close. When a third shot came so close I could feel the percussion from its passage, I suddenly

40

concluded that someone was shooting at me, and I dived for the ground.

As I hit the dirt (not to be confused with biting the dust), a man emptied his gun in my direction. He had never seen me; he simply was shooting at sounds. Evidently his philosophy of hunting was "There are deer in the woods somewhere. If I shoot enough bullets in their direction, I might get one."

What an inefficient and dangerous way to hunt! Yet I have heard hundreds of speakers who apparently have a similar philosophy: "There are kids everywhere who need to hear the Gospel. If I just shoot enough information in their direction, I'm bound to communicate something." This philosophy is just as dangerous and ineffective in communication as it is in hunting.

Hunters will be successful only if they know exactly what they're after, take aim at that single target, and exclude everything else—likewise with speakers. You must know precisely what you are aiming at. Through our Dynamic Communicators Workshops I have taught the principles of communication to thousands of students across the country. The response to these workshops is unanimous. Every aspect of the workshop is appreciated and considered helpful, but students report that the most valuable skill they learn is how to communicate with crystal-clear focus.

The single most important factor in communication is focus. You must know what the objective of your talk will be, and you must be clear about how you are going to achieve that objective. Unfortunately, most talks are prepared by making a list of all the things we want to say (loading a gun with bullets) and then trying to say all of them within the allotted time (shooting indiscriminately into the woods).

There is a desperate need for focus in communication. We did a survey that revealed that over seventy percent of the people who leave Sunday school classes, youth meetings, and church services have no idea what the speaker was trying to say. That is appalling. Yet the saddest statistic was revealed when we interviewed the speakers. Over half of the *speakers* had no idea what they were trying to say. Both groups could identify some of the stories and Scripture used, but neither group could identify *why* the talk was given. To what end were the stories told? What was the target?

On the first night of our Dynamic Communicators Workshop, I ask the students to prepare a five-minute speech and a one-sentence objective (or purpose) for that speech. Before each presentation, students give me a piece of paper on which they have written their objective (the purpose/focus of their talk). When each talk is finished, I ask the listeners in the audience to write down what they thought was the speaker's objective. Most of the time they have no idea. Some write down objectives entirely different from the speaker's objective; some write down the subject or a significant point. But they miss the main point of the talk. Why? Because there was no point. Aim at nothing and you will hit it every time.

Occasionally a student at one of our seminars will object to giving a five-minute talk. The argument is that they usually speak for thirty minutes and don't see the value of five-minute practice. My response is, "If you can't say it in five minutes, you won't be able to say it in a half hour." This response is based on some wise advice given years ago: If you can't state the purpose of your talk in a single clear sentence, you are either trying to say too much or you don't know what you are talking about. Not having a clear objective is about as effective as spraying the woods with bullets, hoping to hit a deer.

The effectiveness of any talk you give is determined before you ever open your mouth. You may resist the effort it takes to apply the principles taught in this book. You may think it isn't worth the time or work. You may be tempted to skip or breeze lightly over these chapters. Don't! Without exception, every student who took the time and effort to apply these principles discovered that it is worth it. Every student who endured the pain of refining each talk to a razor-edge has testified that the effort revolutionized his or her effectiveness as a communicator.

This book will give you the basics you can use during preparation that will help you focus your talk and give it power. You may be entertaining and witty; you may even be interesting. But you will never be effective unless you know exactly what you want to accomplish with your talk and thoroughly plan your strategy for achieving that goal. If you know your objective so clearly that you can write it in a simple sentence, you can strategically plan a talk so that your audience gets the message loud and clear.

The framework for that planning involves a strategy I have named the SCORRE method. This strategy is designed to do two things. First, it forces you to narrow the objective of your speech to a pinpoint focus. Second, it helps unleash your creativity, enabling you to use all available resources to bring that speech to life. Even you will want to listen to your speech with interest from beginning to end! If you follow this process, your audience will listen because you know how to make them listen, and they will know your objective because you know your objective.

The two most important characteristics of a good communicator are the ability to communicate with crystal-clear focus and the skill to take the audience along. The two basic functions of the SCORRE method are designed to help you develop those characteristics in your communication. The SCORRE method forces the speaker to choose a single focus for the talk and provides a framework for logic that forces the speaker to make sense. These are the elements of the SCORRE acronym:

Subject
Central Theme
Objective
Rationale
Resources
Evaluation

The SCORRE method helps you focus your speech by first identifying the *subject*. It sharpens that focus even further by narrowing the subject to a *central theme*. The process helps you pinpoint a clear *objective,* which can be written in a single sentence. Then it provides a framework to expand on that objective by developing a logical, supporting *rationale*. Sparkle and excitement are added to your talk by the creative development and proper use of available *resources*. The SCORRE method allows for constant *evaluation* that assures whether or not you hit your target. At first the SCORRE method seems time-consuming and difficult. But using the process assures that you "SCORRE" with every talk. As you practice, SCORREing your talks will become second nature.

Use this chapter most effectively by preparing an upcoming speech as you read. There is space provided for you to actually work your talk through the process. If you are committed to becoming a better communicator, let's begin by preparing your next talk right now.

CHOOSING A SUBJECT: PICK A CARD, ANY CARD

The process of preparing a speech is like pouring a ton of ideas into a funnel. At the mouth of the funnel are all of our experience and knowledge and a million possibilities from which to choose. The first step when preparing a speech is to choose a single subject from the endless possibilities. This is the beginning of the focusing process. The chosen subject represents a broad area that forms the basis of a speech. In choosing a subject, limitations are determined by asking the following questions.

What Are the Needs of My Group?

I remember watching a youth leader conduct a Sunday school meeting as several of his students wept quietly. Curious, I asked one of the girls what was troubling her. She revealed that there had been a terrible accident that week that had taken the lives of two of their friends. The entire youth group was struggling with this tragedy and the youth leader had simply conducted the lesson for the day. If there ever was a time to recognize and respond to a specific need in a group, this was it. The lesson for the day could not meet their needs. This was a time to deal with the emotions and questions raised by what had happened. I would never suggest that we avoid lesson plans, but the needs of your audience must always be considered, even from the beginning stages of preparation. Good lesson plans are designed with many of those needs in mind. As you choose a subject, ask several questions that will help you effectively meet the needs of your group.

- Who are they? Are they from different churches, gathered for a conference or retreat? If so, the excitement level and anticipation will be much different than if the audience is the same twenty kids who attend your regular youth meeting. The definition of your audience will affect the subject of your speech as well as your delivery.

- Who are they now? Maybe your answer to the first question was, "They are just my usual youth group." But who are they now? Yesterday's excited, energetic group can be today's lethargic, tired complainers. Kids' moods can be greatly influenced and changed by the events of the day or week—a death in the family, a celebration or upcoming prom, even the weather. A skillful and wise communicator will observe and recognize these changes and make the necessary adjustments.

- What do they expect? Once again, expectations depend on the circumstances. Kids at a retreat or conference will anticipate a unique and entertaining program. On the other hand, your Sunday morning class may expect a routine hour (and even brace themselves for boredom). Through the years we have conditioned young people to expect mediocrity by giving them mediocre programs. (Chapter 9 deals with raising kids' level of expectation from apathy to excitement.)

- What do they need? A man stepped into a doctor's office, and the doctor said, "I've been expecting you."

The man opened his mouth to speak, but the doctor interrupted, "Come over here. I have just what you need."

In spite of his patient's protests, the doctor injected medicine into the man's arm. "Now that wasn't so bad, was it?" exclaimed the doctor.

"No, it wasn't bad," said the man, "but I just stopped in to empty your wastebasket. I'm the new janitor."

The doctor didn't take the time to find out what the man needed. So often we run about dispensing medicine without first finding out our patients' needs. We do a great disservice to our kids when we blindly work our way through lesson plans developed by someone who has never laid eyes on our students. We allow practical moments of teachability to slip into eternity.

No wonder many of today's young people think Christianity is irrelevant. We often teach Christian principles in the order they appear in a lesson book, rather than being sensitive to the specific needs of our kids and relating how our faith can meet those needs.

Have I Been Directed to Speak on a Specific Subject?

Many churches or organizations assign a subject to a guest speaker. For example, if the speech is part of a series on dating, dating is the subject. If you are invited to be a guest speaker, keep the subject within the realm of their request.

Do I Know Enough About My Chosen Subject to Speak Intelligently?

A speaker always should know about his or her topic; kids as well as adults can see through unintelligent ramblings. If you have been assigned a subject and feel you don't know enough about it, you have several options:

- Accept the offer and research the topic thoroughly

- Decline the offer and recommend another speaker with more knowledge about the subject
- Suggest another topic

If you are tempted to speak to your group on a subject you know little about—don't. Many youth leaders present a variety of topics at a variety of events such as Bible studies, retreats, or Sunday school classes. If time doesn't allow for thorough research, recruit other speakers from the congregation, community, or school. For example, ask a school counselor to speak on the warning signs of suicide, or ask several teenagers to speak about peer pressure. The important point to remember is, an effective speaker knows his or her subject matter.

Is the Subject Consistent with Scriptural Truth?

Whether we are speaking topically (from general biblical truth) or exegetically (dissecting the truth found in a particular portion of Scripture), it is imperative that we are true to the intent of the Scriptures we are teaching. It is unfortunate that many speakers use Scripture only to give credibility to their talk. Or worse yet they twist Scripture to make it fit whatever they are presenting. The Bible is the very source of the truth we teach. We need to treat it with the respect it deserves.

Let's go through the first step in the SCORRE method and choose a subject. Get a piece of paper and a pen. If you are preparing your talk from a specific portion of Scripture, study that passage and write down all the subjects that are presented. Many passages will have more than one possible subject. If you are preparing a topical speech, consider the needs of your audience and write down the subjects that might touch on those needs. It is easy at this point to mistake one burning issue you want to address for the subject of your talk. A pastor once wrote down "the pitfalls of marriage" as the subject of a wedding message he was about to preach. He became confused until he realized that "the pitfalls of marriage" was just one of several points he intended to cover. His real subject was "successful marriage." "Avoiding the pitfalls that destroy marriages" was just one idea that he felt strongly about. Your subject should be expressed in one or two words that are broad enough to encompass the things you want to say. If you struggle, write down all the things you want to say and then ask, what word describes these ideas? What is this about? You may also choose from the following list. Keep it simple. Don't try to dissect the book of Ecclesiastes. Choose a subject with which you are very familiar. You could even prepare a speech on a hobby or your family. Save the more difficult subjects for after you have mastered the SCORRE method. That will allow you to concentrate on learning the SCORRE method. When you have settled on a single subject, write it in the space provided.

Fear	Faith	Self-Control	Love
Christ	Caring	Suicide	Sex
Rabies	Prayer	Disobedience	Drugs
Forgiveness	Depression	Elephants	Heaven
Bible	Witnessing	Easter	Dieting
Atonement	Confession	Dandruff	Music
Occult	Worship	Christianity	Discipleship
Christmas			

The subject for my speech is: _____

CHOOSING A CENTRAL THEME: COULD YOU BE MORE SPECIFIC?

The second step in the SCORRE method is to choose a single aspect of the subject as a central theme. The theme must be brief and clear and usually is expressed in a phrase. Here are some possible themes for the subject "fear":

Remedies for fear
Identifying fear
Coping with fear
The effects of fear

The subject "occult" could have central themes such as the following:

Identifying the occult
Dangers of the occult
Origins of the occult
Practices of the occult

Notice how the theme determines the broadness of a speech's content. The purpose of this step in the process is to narrow the subject to a manageable amount of information. Most speakers err on the side of trying to say too much. The central theme helps ration the number of bullets you will shoot. If a central theme is "the effects of fear," the body of a talk would deal only with the effects of fear. This talk would have a narrower scope than one with the central theme of "coping with fear." "Coping with fear" could include content dealing with the effects of fear, identifying fear, or even remedies for fear. The central theme is a broad description of the content. At this point in the SCORRE method, you have not yet determined the objective (purpose) of your talk. However, a good central theme will hint at the objective to your talk. If your central theme is "coping with fear" we can be pretty certain that your "objective" will be a talk that instructs on how to cope with fear. If you already have an inkling of the objective, be sure your theme is broad enough to encompass it.

Now in the space provided, once again write the subject you previously chose. Then write some possible themes (like those in the "fear" example) that express single aspects of your subject.

The subject for my speech is: _____

Possible themes (Keep it brief—two or three words): _____

_____

_____

_____

Considering the needs of your audience, the scope of the Scripture you have chosen, and the limitations of your knowledge, choose one of the themes. This will be the focus of your talk.

My central theme is: _____

CLARIFYING YOUR OBJECTIVE: WHAT ARE YOU TRYING TO SAY?

Clarifying your objective is the most difficult, yet important, aspect of preparing a speech. But don't give up now! Your effort to see this through could pay off for the rest of your life. Get a cup of coffee or an injection of caffeine, take a brisk walk around your Toyota, and dig in.

Determining your objective is of primary importance for effective communication. Unfortunately, too many speeches are based on a subject or theme with little thought given to the purpose. In other words, many speakers know what they want to talk about, but they never answer the question *why*. Because of this error, the subject or theme is too broad, and the speech is aimless and boring.

Up to this point, you have been bringing to a sharp focus what you are going to *talk about*. Now you will clarify exactly what you want to accomplish in your speech. This step answers the question, "Why am I giving this talk?" An understanding of what you want to accomplish enables you to articulate that objective in a simple sentence. This objective statement will be composed in four steps.

Step #1: Write a Propositional Statement

The proposition is a simple statement that makes the transition from the content of the talk to the purpose of the talk. It is stated in a clear, simple sentence that always follows a specific form and perfectly summarizes the purpose of your message. There are two basic kinds of propositions:

1. The obligatory proposition
2. The enabling proposition

The obligatory proposition accompanies a speech of persuasion. This talk is designed to move your group to take action, make a commitment, or consider belief.

The enabling proposition will be for a talk that gives instruction or direction. It will show the student how to do something or how to understand a concept.

The form for writing each of these propositions is purposely rigid. It is designed this way to keep you focused and logical. It is impossible to prepare a rambling meaningless talk if you stick to the form. Keep in mind that these are not the exact words you will use when you deliver the talk. They are like the foundation to a beautiful building. You don't see it, but because it exists the building will be sound and attractive. There will be more on this later.

The form for writing an obligatory proposition looks like this:

Every _____ should _____

The first step in developing a proposition is determining to whom you will address your remarks. For example, if your proposition reads, "*Every* Christian *should* love his or her neighbor," the word immediately following the word "every" indicates that the speaker will be addressing the Christians in the audience. If your remarks were directed to the general audience you might use the word *person* instead: "*Every* person *should* love his or her neighbor."

Don't try to say something for everybody in the audience. A speech directed to a group with a particular need will be more effective for everyone in the audience than one that tries to scatter a little truth for everyone (the old shotgun approach again).

The form for writing an enabling objective looks like this:

Every _____ can _____

If you chose the same subject of love, this proposition would read, "*Every* Christian *can* learn to love his or her neighbor."

This would be a very different talk from the obligatory example above. In this talk you will be giving instructions on how to love your neighbor. The obligatory talk would be designed to give reasons why Christians should love their neighbor.

Here are some other examples of obligatory propositions:

- "Every teenager should establish moral guidelines in his or her life." This speech shows "why" teenagers should establish moral guidelines.
- "Every person should learn to ride an elephant." This speech shows "why" a person should learn to ride an elephant.

The next propositions are for enabling speeches:

- "Every teenager can learn how to set moral guidelines in life." This is a speech showing teenagers "how" to set moral guidelines.
- "Every person can learn to ride an elephant." This is a speech showing "how" a person can learn to ride an elephant.

Now it's time to work on your speech. Determine to whom you will be speaking. If you will address everyone in the group, write the word "person" after "every." If you will address all believers, write "believer" in this space. Next determine whether your speech will be one of enablement or one of obligation. If it is an enabling speech, circle the word "can"; if it is an obligatory speech, circle the word "should." Fill in the following blanks, and write a propositional statement for your central theme.

The subject for my speech is: _____

My central theme is: _____

My propositional statement is: _____

Every _____ should/can _____
                              (Choose only one)

Step #2: Question the Proposition

To further develop your objective, you must question the proposition you just wrote. If your proposition is one of obligation, then you must ask, "Why?" If yours is an enabling proposition, then you must ask, "How?" This is exactly the way we respond to such challenges in life. If I walked up to you and said, "You should leave the room," you would ask, "Why?" If I said, "You should be able to recognize an elephant," you would ask, "Why?"

If I looked you right in the eye and said, "You can learn to love your neighbor," your natural response would be, "How can I learn to love my neighbor?" If I said, "You can learn to ride an elephant," you would ask me to show you "how."

In summary, obligatory propositions lead to the question "why" and enabling propositions lead to the question "how."

If your speech is to logically address your proposition, then the body of your obligatory speech must answer the question "why," and your enabling speech must answer the question "how." Other questions, such as where, when, and what, are answered in the body of the speech. Assume, for example, that you have chosen the enabling proposition "Every person can learn to ride an elephant." The natural question for the proposition is *how*. The steps taken to learn this skill might be as follows: (1) Go to the main tent of the circus at 10 A.M. on Friday; (2) ask for Ralph the elephant man; and (3) sign up for lessons. The questions when? with whom? and take what action? are answered within the body of the speech. They all fall under the broader question "How can I learn to ride an elephant?" Asking why or how of your proposition will lead you automatically to the logical body of your speech.

Step #3: Answer the Question "Why" or "How" with a Phrase That Uses a Key Word

The final step in preparing an objective statement is to answer the question why or how with a phrase that contains a key word.

When you are using an obligatory proposition, this response phrase begins always with the words *because of* or *for*. Here is an example:

Proposition: Every *Christian* should *learn to love his or her neighbor*

Response: *because of* the commands given by Christ.

"Every Christian should learn to love his or her neighbor" is the obligatory proposition. It anticipates the question "Why should I learn to love my neighbor?" The phrase "because of the commands given by Christ" fully answers the question and contains the key word "commands." In this talk, each of the points will be one of the commands that Christ gave encouraging us to love our neighbors.

Let's look at another example.

Proposition: Every *Christian* should *learn to love his or her neighbor*

Response: *for** two reasons.

The proposition remains the same as before: "Every Christian should learn to love his or her neighbor." But in this case the answer to the question *why* has broader possibilities. In the previous objective sentence, the key word limited the scope of the talk to the commands given by Christ. Because this speech uses *reasons* as the key word, its scope can be much more broad. It could include, but is not limited to, the commands given by Christ. Any truthful reason is valid for this speech.

When you are using an enabling proposition, the response phrase always begins with the word *by*. Now let's analyze responses to enabling propositions.

Proposition: Every *parent* can *be more effective*

Response: *by* developing two communication skills.

The enabling proposition "Every parent can be more effective" anticipates the question "How can a parent be more effective?" The response "by developing two communication skills" leads the speaker deeper into the talk. Now the "how" can be explained as the speaker focuses on the key word: skills.

*The word *for* is used only when *reasons* is chosen as a key word. (See p. 56 for a discussion of key words.)

Here is another example:

Proposition: Every *Christian* can *find peace*

Response: *by* trusting in three promises of God.

Once again, the response "by trusting in three promises of God" answers the "how" question presented in the proposition "Every Christian can find peace." The key word "promises" leads the speaker into developing his or her talk around the three promises that lead a Christian toward finding peace.

The key word is always a plural noun that embodies the ultimate focus of your message—the very heart of your speech. Words such as *guidelines, consequences,* or *blessings* could be key words. The main points of your message will be divisions of your key word. For example, main points to the key word *blessings* could be home, health, happiness, and so forth. (These main points are called the *rationale.* Constructing the points of your speech is explained in the next section.) Look at the following illustration. Notice again that responses to the question *why* (obligatory propositions) begin with the words *because* or *for;* responses to the question *how* (enabling propositions) begin with *by.* Notice also the examples of key words that can be used with the responses.

Type of Speech	Question	Response	Key Words
Obligation	Why?	Because of . . .	Rules Commands Scripture Advantages Reasons Truth
Enabling	How?	By following the . . . By obeying the . . . By understanding the . . .	Steps Principles Instructions Rewards Examples Blessings

Objective statements are complete once the key words have been added. Following are examples of objectives for speeches of "obligation." Notice the key words in parentheses.

Every _Christian_ should _love his or her neighbor_
because _of the_ (commands) _given in Scripture._
Key Word

Every _Christian_ should _love his or her neighbor_
because _of the_ (rewards) _that await those who do._
Key Word

Every _person_ should _learn to ride an elephant_
because _of the_ (advantages) _over walking._
Key Word

Every _person_ should _learn to ride an elephant_
for _three reasons._
Key Word

Here are some examples of objectives for "enabling" speeches. Notice the key words in parentheses.

Every _person_ can _learn to ride an elephant_
by _following these easy_ (steps).
Key Word

Every _Christian_ can _learn to love his or her neighbor_
by _understanding the_ (principles) _of neighborly love._
Key Word

Every _Christian_ can _learn to love his or her neighbor_
by _following the_ (examples) _set by Christ._
Key Word

Every _Christian_ can _learn to love his or her neighbor_
by _following the_ (instructions) _set forth in Scripture._
Key Word

Now, if you have followed the whole procedure you are ready to take the most important step in preparing your talk. Using the material you already have developed, and following the process explained above, write the objective sentence that expresses the purpose of your talk. Review these rules carefully and refer back to them often as you prepare your objective sentence.

1. Choose either an obligatory or an enabling proposition.
2. Fill in the first blank with a word descriptive of your audience.
3. If your speech is enabling, circle the word *can;* if it is an obligatory speech of persuasion, circle the word *should*.
4. Circle the correct question for your proposition. Remember that obligatory responses are interrogated with the question *why;* enabling responses are interrogated with the question *how*.
5. Choose the proper words to begin your response. If your speech is enabling, you will choose the word *by*. If your speech is obligatory you will choose either *because of* or *for*.
6. Write your response in the second blank. This response must include a descriptive plural noun (key word) that describes the points you will use to drive home your objective.

Every _____ should/can _____

Why/How? _____

because of/for/by _____ (_____) _____ .
                                    Key Word

If this statement is clear and concise, if it contains all the elements we have covered, if you can understand it, and it is exactly what you want to accomplish, then the next step is to break out the champagne, balloons, and whistles (Christian champagne, Baptist balloons, and Wesleyan whistles, of course!). The most difficult, yet important, part is over. You have just clarified your objective. Go ahead and party for a little while, then let's look at how to build a logical case that can help you achieve the objective you just wrote.

Don't give in to that little voice whispering, "This is too much work." I have seen these principles applied by professional entertainers, youth workers, pastors, and business executives. Without a single exception, those who have made the effort to submit their talks to this process have seen dramatic changes in their communication. I am convinced that, subconsciously, most of us have some objective to each of our talks. Unfortunately, most of the time that objective is "I hope they like me," or "I hope I give a good speech," or "I hope they laugh." All of those subconscious objectives are honorable desires, but only as means to an end. Communication that is entertaining changes lives. Entertainment without communication is just entertainment. As youth workers, we have an important message to present. We have a clear-cut objective that is a matter of life and death. If our goals and objectives never go any farther than just pleasing our audiences, then we cease to be ministers. At best we become entertaining babysitters, and at our worst we use the response of our teenagers to meet our own ego needs.

When I presented the SCORRE method to a friend who has been in youth work for many years, he resisted. But as he compared his talks to this process, he saw that many of them were vague and aimless. So he agreed to use the SCORRE method when he prepared his next presentation. He called the youth pastor who had invited him to speak at one of his meetings and asked, "What would you like to accomplish as a result of my being there?"

After some discussion the youth worker replied, "I can't get my kids to commit themselves to anything. I would like you to give a speech that would challenge them to join a small group that would study true discipleship. I've been unsuccessful in doing this. Perhaps you can help."

Once they determined how they would give the group an opportunity to respond to this challenge, my friend hung up and began working on his speech. His subject was "discipleship." His central theme was "steps to becoming a disciple." His objective statement read, "Every individual can become a living disciple of Christ by following three simple steps." The steps included: "Understand what discipleship means; commit yourself to becoming a disciple; act on your commitment by signing up for the discipleship class."

When I called my friend after he had delivered his speech, he said, "You know, Ken, at first I was disappointed. I didn't get as many laughs as I usually get." (This was because he had left out stories and illustrations that were funny, but did not contribute to his objective.) "The kids didn't seem to respond with the enthusiasm that usually greets my speeches; however, both the youth director and I were overwhelmed when, at the end of my talk, eighteen students walked right past the refreshment table (a miracle) to sign up for the discipleship class."

He had accomplished his objective. That's what good communication is all about. When we don't take the time to set an objective, far too often our objective becomes simply to impress our audience by being entertaining and clever. It might work, but to what end? It's more important to determine a worthy goal that brings young people into the kingdom and into a closer walk with our Lord. We still can use entertaining, humorous stories in our speeches, but we selectively use stories that lead the listener to the objective. The SCORRE method works. It hurts, but it works. And those who commit themselves to using the process find it well worth every minute.

As you practice you will be able to determine your objective much faster. It never gets "easy," but then excellence is never easy. You may change your mind several times before you settle on the right objective or find the most effective key word. But what a sense of freedom and purpose when you stand in front of your kids knowing exactly what you want to say and why you want to say it—confident that they will understand what you said and have an opportunity to act on what they heard. Many will remember the message long after they leave the room.

DEVELOPING YOUR RATIONALE: WHAT ARE THE MAIN POINTS OF YOUR MESSAGE?

Developing the subject, central theme, and objective is extremely important because it forces us to zero in on the topic and purpose of our speech. The next step in the SCORRE method is developing the *rationale*, or the main points of the talk. This is the foundation of logic that will lead the listener to the objective of the speech. Those main points of logic must be tied directly to the key word. If the key word is *commands*, then the main points will be specific commands. For example, look at this objective statement:

Every _Christian_ should/can) _learn to love his or her neighbor_ because/by) _applying three_ (principles) _of neighborly love._
Key Word

The key word is *principles;* therefore, the body of the speech could include the following principles as rationale:

Principle   1. _Love like you love yourself (Matt. 19:19)_

Principle   2. _Love like God loved you (John 13:34)_

Principle   3. _Love like you like to be loved (the Golden Rule) (Luke 6:31)_

Look at a more humorous example of an objective statement:

Every _person_ should/can _ride an elephant_ because/by _of the_ (advantages) _over walking._
Key Word

Every person should learn to ride an elephant because of three advantages elephant-riding has over walking.

The key word is *advantages.* Therefore, the main points, or rationale, must be a list of advantages.

Advantage   1. _You can see better from up there._

Advantage   2. _The elephant can't step on you up there._

Advantage   3. _Nobody will try to mug you up there._

"Elephants are dangerous" could not be a main point of this speech because it does not express an advantage. Although "elephants are dangerous" is a true statement, it doesn't belong in this speech because it breaks down the logic of your objective. All main points must relate to the key word. Rewrite your objective statement in the space provided:

Every _____ should/can _____

because of/for/by _____ (**Key Word**) _____ .

Rewrite your key word in the appropriate space below, then write at least two main points:

My key word is: _____

My main points are: _____

1. _____

2. _____

3. _____

4. _____

These main points are the rationale for your talk. Double-check to make sure they are singular expressions of your key word. Once again, the points must be logical, and they must be extensions of your key word.

This is where the idea of the "three-point sermon" originated. Unfortunately this idea has deteriorated, and most three-point sermons are really "three-sermon sermons." Every sermon should have only one objective that is illustrated by two or more main points, as previously illustrated.

The rationale represents a clear purpose for your talk and a logical means of achieving that purpose. Now the fun part begins—bringing the talk to life by creatively using available resources!

GATHERING AND USING RESOURCES: FROSTING THE CAKE

As ministers with youth, we have access to unlimited resources—the Word of God, the church, our youth groups, the world around us. Each day we experience twenty-four hours of living from which at least one experience could be used as an excellent illustration. Think of it. If we could learn to recognize and develop just one experience a day, we would have 365 new illustrations each year. Pretty exciting, huh? Especially when compared to the fifteen illustrations we have been using for the past 365 years (three of which we stole from another speaker).

As a comedian I am often asked where I get new material. It comes from the resource of everyday life. You have the same bountiful resource. As communicators dedicated to excellence, we must train ourselves to see and absorb the experiences of life rather than letting them pass us by.

Several times I have taken friends to see Bill Cosby in a live performance. Without fail, when we leave his performance I hear comments like, "Why didn't I think of that?" I think Cosby is a genius because his comedy deals with those funny experiences we all face every day. Bill Cosby takes those everyday experiences, holds them in front of us, and makes us stop to look. Throughout his performance, people in the audience nudge each other and whisper between laughter and gasps for breath, "That's right." Popular shows like *Home Improvement* and *Friends* draw their humor from real-life situations with which we can identify.

If we are to communicate effectively, we must realize that even the most logical speech in the universe will be of no value unless someone listens. Illustrations and anecdotes are the glitter and sparkle that make people want to listen to our message.

Before we use any resource we must ask two questions:

- Will the illustration or anecdote interest the audience?
- Will the illustration or anecdote enhance and support the message?

We must train ourselves to capture the gems of life that surround us and use them to illustrate and enhance our message.

Where do we find these resources? Everywhere. Watching television; driving to work; processing our own emotions and reactions to events; observing our children, the paperboy, the person checking out groceries, people in a worship service; noticing static electricity in a rug, clothing styles, and other people's reactions to our faith. We must train ourselves to observe and participate in all that we read, see, hear, feel, and experience. Don't just rely on illustration books, which are full of other people's illustrations. The occasional personal illustration can carry far more power. When you do use outside illustration sources, bring them to life with a unique twist.

There is one illustration I must have heard a hundred times if I've heard it once. It's probably a fine illustration. However, I was discouraged by its manipulative nature and its, in my opinion, unrealistic ending. (To be honest, I question its credibility.) The illustration describes a beautiful scene where a train trestle crosses a water channel. A loving father and his son live near the tracks. The father is responsible for raising the trestle to allow boats to pass and then lowering it back into position to allow trains to cross safely. We are made well aware of how much the father loves his small son and how they enjoy their rather solitary, simple life.

As the story goes, one day the father hears a train coming and realizes he has failed to lower the trestle. He runs to the control lever and prepares to throw the switch. At that very moment, he looks up and sees his son playing in the gears of the trestle. There is no time to warn him. The choice is simple. If the father is to save the lives of the people on the train, it will cost the life of his beloved son. With tears in his eyes, he throws the switch and watches his son die in the gears. The illustration is used as a comparison to what God did for us.

I am sympathetic to the point of the illustration. Also, I'm sure this story has been meaningful to many people—maybe you have used it. However, the illustration leaves me cold because I am a father. If I had a choice between my child and a train full of strangers, there would be a train full of strangers swimming in the channel. Because of my discomfort with the traditional ending, when I used the story, I would pause as the father stands poised with his hand on the switch. I would ask, "What would you do?" Over ninety percent of my listeners say they would save their son. I agree.

Looking at the illustration from this realistic perspective gives even more meaning to the fact that even though God must have felt just as we do, he gave up his Son for us all! Just a little twist to the ending made me comfortable with the illustration and helped those who had heard it before see it in a new light.

Here are some other examples of illustrations drawn from real life that have been invaluable to me. I recently saw a sign in a jewelry store window that said, "Ears pierced while you wait." Think about that. You most certainly have to wait to get your ears pierced. Under that sign was another one that said, "On Thursdays we pierce them half off." No thank you! This has worked as a humorous support for material on being patient, living in a hectic society, and the stupidity of bureaucracy.

Good reading is an excellent source for illustrations. Short poems can add tremendous power to speeches. Following is the poem "Overheard in an Orchard" by Elizabeth Cheney. This reading effectively illustrates the folly of worry:

> Said the Robin to the Sparrow:
> "I should really like to know
> Why these anxious human beings
> Rush about and worry so?"

Said the Sparrow to the Robin:
"Friend, I think that it must be
That they have no heavenly Father
Such as cares for you and me."

Everything we read and experience provides us with possible illustrations. So how can we remember these experiences and use them in speeches? Following are some ideas.

Learn How to Observe

We have become so obsessed with doing that we go through life rushing from task to task without seeing what is going on around us. We must discipline ourselves to stop, look, and listen. Try this experiment. Make tomorrow a day that you will try to observe all that happens to you. As a part of the experiment, carry a notebook with you all day. You need not record everything that happens, but you must record those things that move you emotionally or in some way stand out from the norm: the harshness of a harried mother jerking her child through the supermarket, the impatience of the man who cut you off in traffic. If an experience moves you or grabs your attention in some way, it's very likely to move other people as well. That's what good illustrations are made of. If it makes you laugh, if it makes you angry, if it makes you sad, if it makes you happy—in short, if it moves you—grab your pen and write it down. At the end of the day, review what you have experienced. Scratch out the incidents that have lost their punch and keep the ones that still evoke emotion as you read them. You will have several potentially powerful illustrations that you would have missed if you had just blundered blindly through the day. Learn to observe what is going on around you!

Choose a Method to Record Your Ideas

In an article I wrote on becoming a better speaker, I stated that two of the greatest tools a great communicator always should have are a pad of paper and a pencil. My way of making a living depends on acquiring new illustrations and material. It does no good to sensitize our minds to observe the wonderful things happening all around us unless we remember them long enough to use what we have observed.

If your mind is anything like mine, you can forget an incident within a few minutes. When some special experience happens, I am so taken with its potential as an illustration, the possibilities burn like a fire in my mind. Sixty seconds later, all that remains is the dusty residue of old ashes and the distinct awareness that a potentially great illustration has gone to its reward. Am I unique? I don't think so. How many times have you been introduced to someone only to realize moments later you already have forgotten his or her name?

Anyone who has enough taste to purchase this book is brilliant! You have mental capabilities that hold great potential for creative and dynamic communication. Don't waste one single brain cell trying to remember those wonderful tidbits that come your way. Instead, write them down immediately, and save all that genius for creative preparation of the greatest speeches in the world. One of the greatest minds of all time, Albert Einstein, wrote down even the smallest thoughts. He once explained that he never tried to remember anything he could look up (including his home phone number). If Einstein found it practical to write things down, then perhaps we could benefit as well.

As a youth worker dedicated to better communication, never ever go anywhere without a pad and pencil. Use them at every opportunity. Write down not only what you observe, but the ideas those observations stimulate in your mind. Write down the ideas for talks you believe those observations would help you deliver.

Keep a pad of paper and a pencil by your bed. Some of my best ideas come as I am waiting to go to sleep. A word of caution here. Whenever you are half asleep and taking notes, be sure to write your ideas out in detail. One of the side effects of the genius you and I possess is the ability to forget why we wrote what we wrote. This is especially true at bedtime. I remember waking with a splendid idea one night after a dream. I grabbed a pencil, scribbled a note on the pad beside my bed, and fell into a peaceful slumber, knowing it was preserved for posterity and the benefit of the whole world. I woke in the morning to see the word "chicken" scrawled on a piece of paper with no recollection of what it meant or where it came from. All I could remember was that it had been a great idea the night before. Even though it takes a little time and effort, write your observations and inspirations in enough detail so that when you look at them again you will see more than a chicken staring back at you.

Some speakers prefer to carry a small recorder with them. They dictate into a recorder whenever an idea pops into their mind. This is especially helpful if you are one of those who gets inspiration in the middle of the night. You don't have to turn on the lights and then figure out which end of the pencil is the eraser. The only thing more frustrating than trying to figure out the significance of the word "chicken" written the night before is trying to read a whole page of excellent ideas written in eraser. But there are pitfalls with using a recorder. Once in the middle of the night, I dictated an elaborate illustration into the television remote control. Another drawback of a recorder is that until the tape is transcribed, it can be difficult to locate the illustration you are looking for.

File Illustrations So You Can Find Them

Regardless of how you choose to record those gems of wisdom that bombard you daily, the next step is to file them in such a way that will be useful to you later. For example, years ago I pulled a prank in a restaurant that has become a mainstay illustration. As my family and I sat down, a surly waitress with the disposition of a linebacker who has just had his head stepped on threw our menus on the table and demanded, "What do you want?" She took our order without ever smiling. It was as though we were being punished for coming to the restaurant. In my pocket I had a small puppet made of rabbit fur. When manipulated properly and accompanied by the proper squeaks, it looked so much like a live rat that I almost could fool myself.

Hoping to brighten the waitress's day and bring a smile to her lips, I hid the little rascal beneath my salad and hung its tail over the edge of the bowl. When she returned, I grabbed the tail and made the puppet run screeching up my arm and down my shirt. The waitress caused a lot of destruction as she fled the room. Tables and plates flew everywhere. I had no intention of scaring her, but I did. Likewise when we came in, the manager had no intention of kicking us out, but he did.

At the time the event seemed rather foolish, but as time passed I shared the experience, and people found it delightful. Because it is a story that can be demonstrated as well as told, it quickly became a favorite. I wrote the experience almost word for word. Later I reduced it to a few phrases to remind me of the key points in the illustration. Finally, "rat" became the word to remind me of the entire illustration.

As you begin your own file, at first it may be necessary to write your illustrations in considerable detail, but once you are comfortable with them, file the illustrations under a single word. "Wedding" may be the word that brings to mind an incident that happened at a wedding. "Blind boy" may be the words that trigger your memory of a touching illustration about a blind boy's experience.

It is a good practice to carry a small file of familiar illustrations such as this with you. A page or two of these dependable quickies can come in handy when you are asked to speak on short notice. This file could be as small as a single piece of paper. The only space required is enough room to write the word "rat." You can compile your list alphabetically, topically, or chronologically as they come to you. Whatever your choice, you end up with a mini traveling file of illustrations that can be a lifesaver.

Cross-reference Your Illustrations

The next step is to cross-reference these illustrations by topic. When you prepare a specific talk you can quickly review only those illustrations that apply to the topic you are trying to illustrate. The rat illustration, because of its humor and impact, is useful in many situations. I have cross-referenced it under speeches on belief, fear, and faith. The rat story illustrates the principle, what you believe affects your behavior. The surly waitress believed it was a rat, and her body responded as though that were true. The story also illustrates our irrational fears. When I give motivational talks to service people like waitresses and flight attendants, the same illustration is used as an example of how not to treat customers. Sometimes I simply tell the story as an attention-getter. If I actually use the little puppet, it never fails to get attention!

You should also keep a more permanent topical file. If you are preparing a speech about love, you should be able to flip through a topical folder on "love" and find a number of words listed under that heading. Each word should represent an anecdote or illustration. Longer and less familiar illustrations will be filed here as well. This file will contain articles ripped from magazines, detailed observations you have made from your own experience, and cross-references to other files where illustrations of love might be found.

If you have a computer, you can design or buy a program that will list these headings for you. Under "topics" and "Scripture," you can file dozens of key catchwords that represent illustrations you have gathered. A touch of a key can display the illustration written in detail if you forget what the word represents.

Accumulate and Develop Material

After diligently writing down daily events, you will have collected some stories that you never have used. The process of accumulating and developing material requires dedication, concentration, and time. But the payoff is tremendous because the material adds life and personality to your talks. All great communicators master the art of finding and filing illustrations.

If you travel extensively and constantly speak to different audiences, you only need a few illustrations. If you speak to the same audience often, you'll soon use your candy-stick illustrations and will need to tap into the resources around you.

On January 28, 1986, six crew members and one school teacher left a launch pad at the Kennedy Space Center. Less than two minutes into the flight, the space shuttle exploded into a ball of flame, while a stunned nation watched.

After my own sorrow and shock subsided, I wrote down the details of the incident and the emotions and thoughts it stirred in my soul. The result was an excellent illustration that at the time almost everyone could relate to. But eventually a whole new talk emerged. The title of the talk was "The Worst Tragedy on Earth." It illustrated how, as sad and horrible as the Challenger tragedy was, there was a worse tragedy. The seven astronauts died at the pinnacle of their careers. Their sacrifices and commitments had propelled them toward the realization of their goals. Their deaths, even in the moment of glory, were indeed a tragic and sad event, but a worse tragedy is a life lived without commitment or goals. The aimless soul who finds himself or herself at the end of life without having reached out, without having made peace with God, without having set goals, is so much more tragic. The newspaper headline telling of a drunk teenager driving off the road, thus ending his life, is much more tragic than the space shuttle story. A drive-by shooting that causes the death of a teenage gang member is representative of a greater tragedy.

Keep in mind that an illustration doesn't have to be big to be good. The week after the horrible bombing of the federal building in Oklahoma City, pulpits and platforms were deluged with sermons using that disaster as an illustration. But perhaps some of the most effective illustrations were those like I heard in a message delivered by Candie Blankman. She related how the news made her want to get home and hold her own children and express one more time how much she loved them. She rushed home and burst through the door wanting only to hold her children and reaffirm her love to them. But they met her with selfish demands, whining complaints, and vicious sibling fighting. They wouldn't even let her say the words she wanted to say. They refused to listen to her, to feel or respond to her compassion. Few parents know the agony of losing a child in a disaster like that in Oklahoma City. But Candie had touched a raw nerve with the parents in that room by using the Oklahoma bombing as a springboard for a more powerful and practical illustration with which every parent could identify: the pain of loving without getting love in return.

In summary, look for illustrations everywhere. Learn to observe all that happens around you. Record all that you observe. Use illustrations to support your statements and bring life to your talks.

Now that you have chosen a subject, narrowed it to a central theme, developed an objective, organized your rationale in a logical manner, and added life to the talk with resource illustrations, it is time to evaluate your speech.

EVALUATING YOUR PREPARATION: CHECK IT OUT

Evaluating speech preparation is like straining your talk through a filter to remove the impurities. To evaluate, run your roughly prepared speech through these questions.

1. Did I follow the steps in the SCORRE method?
2. Have I considered the needs of my audience?
3. Does my speech apply to the kids' needs?
4. Is the subject of my speech one that interests the kids?
5. Do I know what I'm talking about, or do I need more research?
6. Does my speech fit the guidelines I've been given? Does it correspond with the theme of the event or the assigned topic?

7. Has my objective been written clearly? Do I know exactly what I want to accomplish with my audience?
8. Are my main points of logic (rationale) tied directly to the key word in my objective?
9. Have I limited my rationale to a few points, or have I tried to cover too much material?
10. Have I added life to my speech with interesting illustrations?
11. Are my rationale and objectives consistent with the truth found in Scripture?

Sometimes evaluating your speech preparation may require you to rethink your whole objective; other times it simply helps you clarify and sharpen your talk.

Now you have completed the SCORRE method. You are ready to put the final touches on your speech.

Note: The coverage of the SCORRE method in this book is a condensed overview of a detailed and systematic process. If you want information on the Dynamic Communicators Workshop or other materials dealing with communication, write Ken Davis Productions, P.O. Box 745940, Arvada, CO 80006–5940, or call 1–800/425–0873.

CHAPTER THREE

Tell Me the Old, Old Story

WARNING! If you misuse the method of preparation you have just learned, you can end up sounding like a robot. SCORRE is a method of preparation that determines your objective and the steps you will take to get there. The sentence you have learned to write is like the foundation on which a beautiful building can be built. If you use the same exact words written in your objective to present your message, you may have to put a guard at the door to keep the kids from leaving during your talks. Once the foundation of a building is in place, it is covered up. Then it becomes the anchoring point for the structure that is built on it. It is vital, but not necessarily visible. The SCORRE method has a rigid design to keep you honest and focused. As long as you keep that focus, the possibilities of presentation are limited only by your imagination. SCORRE is a method of preparation, NOT a model of delivery. In this chapter you will learn a few of the various methods that can be used to present a message that is built on a single, solid, objective foundation. Just because you are focused doesn't mean you have to be boring and predictable. We ought to be constantly searching for innovative ways to communicate truth.

Jesus never spoke without a clear purpose, but he used a variety of methods to get his point across. He used picturesque metaphors and compelling stories to bring truth to an illiterate society. These methods are very powerful in today's culture as well. Today, images and sound bites have replaced the written word as a means of disseminating information. Kids spend much more time watching television than they do reading books. We should never stop encouraging kids to read, especially the Word of God, but because many of them don't read, we must vary the methods we use to reach them.

CONSIDER ALL THE OPTIONS

Let me demonstrate. You have an average youth group with a number of rebellious kids. (Okay, you don't have any rebellious teenagers in your group, but just play along!) Many of them have expressed a fear of turning back to God. They are afraid they have gone too far. They feel God may not want them anymore. At the same time, other members of your group are judgmental toward these rebels and show little compassion. You have been moved by your study of Luke 15. In the story of the prodigal son you see a message of hope that demonstrates God the Father's unconditional love for us as his children.

You determine that your subject is God's love and your central theme is understanding God's love. Then you write an objective and rationale that look like this:

Every person in our youth group can grow closer to Christ by understanding two facts about God's love.
1. God loves you no matter what!
2. God wants you to come home!

Certainly one of the ways this could be presented is to stand in front of your group, creatively announce that tonight you want to talk about two facts that will help the group draw closer to Christ, and deliver a quality two-point message in the classic and perfectly acceptable propositional style. But look at the other options that are available to you.

You can simply read the story as it appears in Scripture and ask questions that will reveal the two truths in your rationale.

If you know the story of the prodigal son well enough, you can tell it in common language, emphasizing the truth you wish to communicate.

You can also tell the story using characters of the present period. The father owns a BMW dealership. The son demands his inheritance and runs away to Las Vegas where he loses everything. When he comes back the father forgives him of everything and throws a big party. Ask your kids what they feel about the story. Ask how they think God feels when one of his children wanders away and then returns. Then read the real account from the Bible.

GET THE KIDS INVOLVED

Use questions that allow the kids to discover the truth you are trying to teach. Have you ever known anyone who deserted their family and ruined their life? Did they come back? Why? Why not? How were they received when they returned? How do you think God feels when we turn our backs on him because we think it would be more fun to just do what we want? How do you think God feels when we come home? What a great time to challenge kids in different stages of rebellion to return to the Father! What an opportunity to show kids that they should be merciful to members of their group who may be in rebellion.

What if you had your group do a role play of this story? Read the account. Then assign one teenager the role of the father, one the role of the prodigal son, another the role of the brother, and make the rest of the group the servants who observe the whole affair. You might even have several kids play the role of the pigs. Have them discuss their feelings about this rich boy eating their food. If you are a father or mother, you could conclude by sharing the love you feel for your children.

If you know an actual story of a wayward son or daughter who returned home and found forgiveness, you could use this story in a compelling way. Ask some stimulating questions about love and grace and then conclude by reading the biblical account of the prodigal son without adding any concluding comments. It may be that some members of your group could give a testimonial of a prodigal experience in their lives. Imagine how long the truth of this passage would last in the minds of your kids if you helped them produce a video that emphasizes the two facts you want them to know.

Each of the above methods of presentation is built on the solid foundation of the same single objective: "Every person in our youth group can grow closer to Christ by understanding two facts about God's love."

DON'T BE AFRAID TO GO FOR THE THREE POINTS

The presentation of truth using the old two- or three-point sermon can be used for some very powerful presentations. Don't be afraid to use it. Just be careful not to overuse it. In the case of the two-point sermon delivery, you actually list the two facts as points of your talk. In the case of the narrative, the facts are revealed in the context of the story. In the role play and ensuing discussion, you design the questions and the role play to reveal the two facts. You can design your meeting in such a way that a simple reading of the passage at the end of your presentation answers the questions you have raised throughout the meeting: "God loves you no matter what you have done! God wants you to come home!"

Once you have the points of truth you want to communicate (rationale) and you know what you want to accomplish with that truth (objective), a world of creative possibilities is at your fingertips. With your focus in mind, use those options to prepare, and you will create memories of life-changing truth that will last in the minds of your kids as long as they live.

CHAPTER FOUR

Take Your Time

Henry is under the gun. Each week he sets aside Tuesday to prepare for his youth meeting on Wednesday night. This Tuesday he had just begun to put his message together when the phone rang. It was the distraught mother of one of his kids. He listened and counseled for thirty minutes and then went back to his study. There was a knock at the door. Some of his old youth group members were back from college and decided to pop in for a moment. An hour and a half later they gratefully thanked Henry for his time and walked out the door. Henry looked at his watch. He was late for the ministerial meeting at the Village Inn. His senior pastor had asked Henry to represent him at this meeting, and now Henry was going to be late. Already behind schedule, he spent the rest of the day trying to catch up. He never got back to working on his message. At 11:30 he dropped into bed, exhausted. The pastor was returning early in the morning and Henry was supposed to pick him up at the airport. Tomorrow's schedule was already full. When was he going to find time to prepare for his youth meeting? As he dozed off, Henry made a mental note to use his lunch hour to work on the message for that evening. It didn't happen. Henry's wife, two of his students, and the pastor had other plans. Henry prepared for his message over dinner that night, putting the final touches on the meeting as he drove to the church, almost rear-ending two cars in the process. That night Henry delivered a mediocre message in the context of a poorly planned youth meeting. He hated doing it this way. He hated even more the fact that it had happened dozens of times before and he knew that it would happen again.

Does this sound familiar? This chapter will show you the steps you can take to get yourself out from behind the eight ball and put you back in control.

PREPARE IN STAGES: TAKE SMALL BITES WITH TIME TO CHEW

One of the most valuable ingredients of any speech is time. Speakers who prepare an entire speech the week it is to be delivered do themselves, their youth group, and their speech a tremendous disservice. The period of time over which you prepare a message is as important as the amount of time you spend preparing the message. Put another way, a speech prepared over a two-hour period on Friday that is delivered on Saturday will not have a fraction of the effectiveness of a speech prepared in stages with the two-hour preparation time spread over two or three weeks. A speech is much like a good wine. The best is that which has had a chance to ferment and age. A good host would never serve a wine that had been in the bottle for only a few days. Likewise, there is no excuse for serving up a message that has not had time to ferment.

There are four stages to any speech, sermon, or talk. The first stage is the idea stage where the speech is just a gleam in your eye. During this stage of preparation you should allow the creative juices to flow; let your mind go free. Nothing should stop your pen from moving. Write all kinds of preliminary ideas on paper: illustrations you want to use, needs you want to meet, a joke you may use to open. You'll probably think of items that need refinement before you can speak on them; write them down in raw form. You'll probably think of items that could get you fired if you speak on them. Write them down. Your goal is a piece of paper covered with free-flowing ideas. A one-person brainstorming session. You may think of a subject or central theme. It may be that some of your rationale or even your objective might come to you. So much the better. You are ahead of the game. The important thing to remember is that in this stage of development, your talk does not have to be in its final shape. It may not have a shape at all. At this stage you are using your preparation time to consider possibilities. These ideas will continue to grow and develop even as you move on to work on other speeches in various stages of development. When thoughts come that fit with other talks, pull out the idea folder for the appropriate speech and add your thoughts to it. Then go back to the talk you were working on. Consider that if you had skipped the idea stage or if you were waiting till the day before your talk to begin preparation, there would be no development at all.

Next comes the skeleton stage. During this stage you work your ideas through the SCORRE process. You write an objective sentence and the points of your rationale. By the end of this stage you've articulated exactly what you want to communicate, and you know how you are going to go about it.

The third stage of preparation is the outline stage. During this stage you add an opening and closing and arrange your illustrations and supportive material to support your rationale and objective. You decide how to start your talk with power, you think through your transitions, and you decide how to close your speech in a way that will move your audience to action. You may want to make notes of areas of the talk you think need to be strengthened. These final touches can be added during the final stage of preparation. In an emergency it would be acceptable to deliver the speech at the end of the skeleton stage, but the excellent communicator would want the speech to go through one more process, the fermentation stage. This is when the speech is allowed to ferment in the quiet cellars of your consciousness. Ideally, every prepared speech should be given at least an additional week to interact with the enzymes of life. During this time you will encounter events and observations that fit perfectly with your speech. You will not be making major changes, but the additions and changes you do make will give your speech its final razor-edge of excellence.

If you don't give your speech time to ferment, those events and observations will pass into oblivion without your ever being aware of their presence. If you allow your speech to ferment, they will become the powerful anecdotes, illustrations, and clarifications that raise your speech above the mediocre. At that point you are ready to serve a vintage message. Here's the really beautiful part. If your senior pastor insists that you help with a mailing by licking envelopes for two days (that will leave a bad taste in your mouth), you will still have a choice of two or three messages that have been exposed to preparation and time. Any of them can be delivered on the spur of the moment with more preparation and power than the old "while you're eating" style of preparation. Even messages that haven't been through the fermentation stage have had time to mature. Any message beyond the skeleton stage will be better than the one prepared at the last minute.

GET AWAY AND GET AHEAD

I know what you are thinking: Where am I going to find the time for such preparation? I'm swamped already. Have you ever wondered where the president of the United States finds the time to accomplish all that needs to be done? Perhaps you have even wondered if he doesn't have a hidden cache of time that is unavailable to you and me. The truth is that we all have the same twenty-four-hour period each day in which to accomplish what we must do. It is how we manage that time that makes the difference. The reason that people with unbelievable workloads have the time to accomplish so much is because they plan ahead. Proper management of your time will allow you to accomplish double what you are doing now with half the hectic stress. The principle of preparing in stages works specifically with the preparation of a speech, but it applies to the other aspects of your life as well. Much of the burnout and stress found in youth work could be eliminated if we learned how to properly manage our time.

The first step in the process is to recognize that there will be an initial price to pay for the freedom you will gain down the road. You may even want to get a pencil and write down this cost. The cost of saving time is . . . time! The wise money manager knows that if he wants to make money over a period of time, he must be willing to invest some money up front. You will never get beyond crisis management until you are willing to invest some time up front on a regular basis. If you are willing to commit to that investment, you can reap wonderful future dividends: You will be a more effective minister and a more accessible spouse as well as a more dynamic communicator. You may have to reprioritize and convince your superiors of the value of this process, but you must take some time to get away (your investment) and get ahead (your reward). I know! We think that if we take a couple of days to get our lives in order, the ministry will fall apart. Not true. Think back to the last time you got sick or were called away by an emergency. Perhaps you were gone several days or even a week. When you returned, it was almost as though you never left (Kind of hard on the ego, huh?). Now, think of the benefits you will receive by getting away for the sole purpose of organizing your life: treat youth meetings, hotter talks, less stress, less guilt, and freedom to really minister to kids.

Are you ready? Here's the plan! Take no less than three days to get away from the phone and all distractions for no other reason than to prepare three complete messages and to put three others in various stages of development. Make the commitment to get away and get ahead. If you have to invite a guest speaker or have the students lead a meeting in order to make this investment possible, do it. Do it on a regular basis. When the unplanned misfortunes of ministry happen and you begin to deplete your savings account of messages, take the time to build the account back up. This way you will never again begin preparing a message in the same week you deliver it. When you return, your usual preparation time can be used much more efficiently. Rather than spending the whole time working on the message you are supposed to deliver in a few days, you will work on several messages, moving each to a new stage of development. The message for the current week will receive the final touches of excellence rather than the frantic effort of total preparation.

Remember the mental commitment you made a few minutes ago? The commitment to get away and get ahead? I can guarantee you this: Once you have tasted the freedom and excellence that comes with this kind of one-ahead planning and preparation in stages, you will never be satisfied with the shoot-from-the-hip message again. Good thing too. Because your kids knew you were winging it all along. Remember: Get away and get ahead (set a date now), prepare in stages, and give your messages the benefit of time.

CHAPTER FIVE

Physical Preparation

A warrior never would go into battle without the weapons necessary to fight. A plumber never would enter a home without the necessary tools and a working knowledge of how to use them. Your weapons and tools are your notes, the room you meet in, the microphone, and the audience. Here's how to use them.

NOTES: USE 'EM OR ABUSE 'EM

There are as many opinions on how to use notes as there are speech instructors. My opinion is that if you have to read your speeches word for word, one of two things is true: Either you have not practiced your speech enough or you are in the wrong business. I never have listened to an interesting speaker who read a speech word for word. One of the greatest preachers I ever listened to typed his sermons word for word, but knew them so well by the time he preached that he referred to them only on occasion. Even when I was a teenager, his messages held my attention.

Adults may sit through a read speech, but kids won't. If you have a youth group who sits still while you read your lessons and sermons, then either you have died and gone to heaven and you just don't know it yet, or your group has died and gone the other way, and you haven't noticed because you were reading at the time.

Write out a rough draft of your speech several days prior to your presentation. Pay close attention to the introduction (the first fifty words) and the closing. Kids decide quickly whether or not they want to listen to the speech. Your introduction will convince them one way or the other. Help move them to action with a powerful conclusion—a memorable story or other method of summary that drives home the objective of your speech. (Chapter 6 explains further details about the first fifty words and conclusion of a speech.) In this rough draft, begin to work on transitions from one point of your rationale to the next.

Closer to the date of your speech, refine your material. Eliminate nonessential items and condense your notes to their final form. For the final form of your notes, write your objective sentence at the top of a piece of paper or on a three-by-five card. Write it large enough so that you will not be tempted to deviate from that single purpose. Keep in mind that when you deliver your talk, you will not use the exact language of your objective. How boring it would be to have a speaker start every speech with the same words. "Every person should or can . . ." Carefully consider the words you will use to express the objective. For instance, "every teenager can stay morally pure by guarding three areas of their life" might be expressed as follows: "At some time each of you has been challenged to live a morally pure life. Two weeks ago I talked about the consequences of immoral living and several of you expressed a desire to keep your life pure. The question is, 'How can I be pure in the face of the pressures and temptations I face each day?' Tonight we will answer that question. I want to show you how you can stay morally pure by guarding three areas of your life." This sets you up perfectly for a speech on how to maintain moral purity in the face of temptation. You should have this wording firmly established in your mind before you step to the platform.

Back to your notes. Beneath the objective, write an outline of the main points of your talk (rationale). Include code words for the illustrations and anecdotes you will use to bring life to your speech. Here is an example of what your final notes might look like:

Objective: Every teenager can get more out of the worship service by taking four simple steps.

Introduction: Pony story

Transition: Objective written word for word in conversational language

Step 1: Come expecting to learn
        a. Little girl's prayer
        b. Magazine quote

Step 2: Sit in the front
        a. Preacher's heart attack
        b. No barriers

Step 3: Take notes
        a. Quote retention figures
        b. Do example exercise

Step 4: Apply at least one thing you learn

Conclusion: There are only two options
        Restate objective

Although this outline won't mean much to you, the reader, each word will remind the speaker of an illustration, quotation, or story that supports the main points. Under Introduction, "pony story" will remind the speaker of a story that will grab the attention of the audience and make them want to hear the rest of the speech.

Under step 2, "preacher's heart attack" is a reminder of a humorous illustration. At this point, the speaker tells his or her group to make the transition to sitting in the front row on Sundays a gradual one. If the whole group were to move from those cherished backseats to the front row in one Sunday, the surprise would quite likely cause the preacher to die from a heart attack.

The second point under step 3 reminds the speaker to lead an exercise that proves that writing something down makes it stick in the memory.

The words under Conclusion remind the speaker to restate the speech's objective and tell a story that indelibly imprints the message in the kids' minds.

The details of each point should be committed to memory. Then you can throw your notes away! If you keep them they should simply serve as a reminder of the next element in your speech. You should be familiar enough with your speech so that you rarely have to refer to your notes. However, when you do find it necessary to refer to your notes,

- Have them handy
- Know them well enough to find your place
- Take the time to get the information you need to cover the next point

A casual glance at your notes to refresh your memory is acceptable. An obvious dependence on notes that continues to leave you confused tells your audience that you are not thoroughly prepared or that you don't want to look at them anymore. Don't allow yourself to be paralyzed with fear that you might miss a point. The truth is that your audience will rarely even know that you missed a point. You are the only one who knew it existed. So relax. If your speech is well prepared, the omission of an illustration or story will not destroy it.

The fewer notes you use, the better. Even when you use a minimum of notes, how you use them affects the dynamics of your presentation. Three-by-five cards seem to be the most unobtrusive. They can be held in your hand easily and don't distract from normal gestures. It is also easier to keep track of your progress by moving your last note card to the bottom than it is to find your place on a large page of notes.

Notes should be a silent partner. Don't bring attention to them by waving them at the audience or digging them out of a pocket. Here are some creative ways I have observed excellent speakers using notes:

- Tape note cards in a Bible or reference book. As you read Scripture verses or passages from the book, you can refer to your notes at the same time.

- Write notes on huge cue cards. Place them in an inconspicuous location in the back of the room. This is not a bad idea; almost all television performers use cue cards.
- Write your basic outline on an overhead or slide projector and allow the group to see your notes with you. This also serves as a visual reinforcement of the truth you are teaching. Just be sure that you reveal the points only as you cover them. Do not put your entire outline up at one time. You will need to memorize the illustrations or anecdotes, or place note reminders of the resources elsewhere. The audience would be distracted if the words "tell the joke about the chocolate cow" were displayed on an overhead projector.
- Tape a three-by-five card to the microphone stand.
- Place notes on a music stand. Position the stand off to one side and slightly in front of you.
- Musicians often tape notes to the top edge of their guitar.

Experiment to find a way of referring to your notes that will be comfortable for you and not obvious or distracting to your audience.

As we learned in chapter 4, our communication often falls short of its fullest potential because we postpone our preparation until the night before or possibly hours before the event. Some speakers have been known to improvise on the spot. (I'm confident no one reading this book has done that!)

Once your first draft of notes is assembled, let the speech ferment in your mind. It's a fascinating process that brings clarity to areas that once were unclear, sparkle to points that once were dull. It is often during this process that you remember experiences or have thoughts, ideas, and inspirations that would add life to your talk. You'll say, "Hey, that will work as a great illustration for Sunday night." If the skeleton of the speech were not already hanging in your mind, some experiences would disappear into oblivion. What a tragedy to not give life experiences time to impact our talks. Prepare your speech far ahead of time and let it ferment. This commitment alone will greatly reduce your need for notes. Time is a prepared speaker's best friend.

During the fermentation period, practice your speech mentally. Think through each phase. Then recite the key portions of your talk out loud. Test it with your tongue.

Many times what we have conceived in our mind or written on paper can be difficult to express out loud with lips and words. It is easy to think about "Capricorns, Cupids, and Catapulting Khaki Camels," but try saying it out loud! If your subject happens to be "Rubber Baby Buggy Bumpers" you are in big trouble. Like word tongue twisters, there are also concept tongue twisters. Many concepts of our faith are much easier to think about than they are to express verbally. So during the fermentation period, pray for wisdom and a personal commitment to the truths you are teaching. Think through your speech and make sure it is possible to verbalize your thoughts. Think to clarify, observe to personalize, and verbalize to make sure your lips are willing and capable of transporting those gems of wisdom from your brain to your audience.

If you apply the concepts of your talk to your own life, a dimension is added to your communication for which no amount of technical skills can compensate. When possible, share the ideas you are contemplating with friends. Since this is a time when your speech will attract ideas like a magnet, keep a pad of paper and a pencil handy and record them all.

Imagine that you are to give your speech in twenty-four hours. Your rough draft, including new ideas and clarifications, has been written. Your mind has had time to cement the ideas and focus on the objective. Sit down and write a final draft of your notes. You may find that some changes and additions are needed. Make those changes now and put them in note form. Practice delivering your speech.

As a teenager on our farm, I loved to rehearse speeches with a milk pail over my head. This gave my voice the resonant sound it would have in a large auditorium. Adding my own sound effects of uncontrollable audience laughter and

applause, I would walk for hours among the cattle, pail over my head, giving speeches and preaching sermons that could sway the masses. (I didn't sway any of the cattle though.)

One day, I wondered why I had never blundered into one of the animals. I took off the pail to find every brown eye in the pasture was on me. They were keeping their distance and they looked very, very puzzled. Maybe they were of a different faith.

Some time later, I managed to get my head through the narrow neck of a milk can. The auditorium in there was magnificent, but the exit wasn't sufficient, and that's another story. The point is that practice leads toward perfection. Whether done into a milk can or in the shower, practice your speech out loud.

Try to practice the speech at least once out loud, preferably to someone who will give you feedback. If you can't find a person to listen or if you don't have a tape recorder, then practice in front of a mirror. Silly and old-fashioned as this might sound, it is a terrific exercise. Professional actors, dancers, and speakers do it all the time. Practice anywhere—in the car, in bed, in the bathroom; it doesn't matter. Go through all the parts of the speech out loud until you feel comfortable with them.

Now make any final adjustments in your notes—and relax. If you have dedicated yourself to the previous steps of preparation, that miraculous mind of yours will continue to work and refine. The result will be a confident and dramatic presentation that accomplishes the objectives it was meant to accomplish. The speech may not be perfect, but it will be a thousand times better than the one you would have given had you waited until the last minute to prepare.

PUTTING IT ALL TOGETHER:
IT LOOKS GOOD ON PAPER, BUT DOES IT WORK?

Now that you have the necessary tools for making a good speech, let's review the SCORRE method and other aspects of preparing a talk from beginning to end.

1. Choose a subject. The first step in preparing a speech is to choose a subject from endless possibilities. Be

sure your subject meets the needs of your audience and interests them as well.

2. Choose a central theme. Narrow your subject to one aspect. For example, if your subject is "friendship," a theme could be "making and keeping friends." Be sure to consider the limitations of your knowledge. Depending on your chosen subject and theme, you may have to research for more facts. Double-check the needs of your audience and be sure the subject and central theme meet those needs.

3. Clarify your objective. Determining a clear objective is vital for effective communication. An objective is a simple sentence that clarifies what you want to accomplish in your speech. You may want to review the steps to writing your objective sentence (see pp. 51–58).

4. Develop your rationale. The main points of a speech are called the rationale. Remember, these points are specific and logical, and they relate to the objective.

5. Gather and use appropriate resources. List all the illustrations and support material you could use with your subject. Depending on how much time you have to work on your talk, you may want to have most of the material readily available. This is the time to research illustrations and data for points that need more clarification.

6. Evaluate your preparation. Answer the eleven questions found on pages 73 and 75. Then move on to add finishing touches to your speech.

7. Write the first draft of your speech. Long before you are to speak, write the first draft of your notes and review the entire speech mentally. Carefully plan for your introduction and closing. Design the transitions from one part of your speech to another. The introduction and closing should be powerful and interesting; the transitions should be

smooth. Verbalize your transitions, opening statements, and closing. Be sure to practice out loud concepts you have not tried to put into words.

8. Allow time for your speech to ferment and purify in your mind. Be aware of new material and ideas that can be added. Write down the thoughts as soon as they occur to you.

9. Refine your talk. Eliminate nonessential material and condense your notes to their final form. At this point you should know the introduction, objective, rationale, and conclusion by memory. Ask a person to listen to you practice your speech out loud. If no one will listen, record the speech with a tape recorder and listen to yourself.

Most speakers will not take the time and effort to complete these preparatory steps. That is why most speakers are mediocre. Even in ancient times, the Greeks evaluated their speeches by using three words: logic, ethics, and rhetoric. They asked themselves, "Is the speech logical? Does it make sense?" It's possible for a speech to be very entertaining and interesting, but to be effective, it must be logical. "Is the speech ethical? Am I practicing what I preach?" This evaluation ensured the Greeks that the principles they were teaching were true. It also challenged them to live by those principles. The word "rhetoric" was used to evaluate the wording and structure of the speech. "Is the speech interesting and oratorically correct?" The logic of the speech was achieved through careful preparation and evaluation. The ethics of the speech were determined by the truth of its content and the life of the speaker. Correct rhetoric could only be achieved by practice.

The same evaluations work as well today as they did thousands of years ago. Apply them to the speech you have just prepared. All that remains is to ask God to work through you. If this preparation seems like too much work, at least try it for your next major speech. If you are like others, you soon will be unwilling to speak without at least making an effort in this direction. Once you see how good preparation enhances your communication, you will be convinced that the effort was worthwhile. Once you learn the procedure, it will become an essential part of every preparation.

PREPARING YOUR ENVIRONMENT: GET THE PIGEONS OUT OF THE CHURCH

Regardless of a speaker's talent, the message and all the effort that went into the speech can be lost if the physical setting is wrong.

When asked to speak after a hayride one fall, I had grave reservations. Usually these gatherings were outside amidst constant distractions, poor lighting, and repeated interruptions. The weather was invariably cold (northern Minnesota), and the atmosphere hyped kids for smooching, not worshiping. On top of all these drawbacks, this particular hayride would be accomplished with real horses, so I would have to watch my step.

The pastor tried to put my fears to rest. He assured me that the meeting was to be held in a barn and that the group was providing a spotlight and a quality sound system. So I agreed to give the speech.

The meeting time came and 200 teenagers fresh off a romantic hayride gathered on bales of hay to listen. Everything was as promised. The lighting was superb and the sound system was one of the best. This audience of rosy-cheeked cherubs seemed eager to hear what I had to say. However, unknown to me, about thirty pigeons also had gathered on the rafters above us. I'm not sure whether they had come to hear me or whether the barn was their usual Saturday night hangout. What I am sure of is this: Pigeons are not welcome at my meetings anymore.

At intervals of about two minutes, one or another of these creatures dropped a pigeon missile into the crowd. Some of these missiles hit my audience, some didn't, but when it came to destroying my efforts at even basic communication, every pigeon missile was right on target.

You may never have to face this kind of environmental distraction, but the environment you speak in may have pigeons of a different kind. You can raise the level of your effectiveness several notches by taking note and correcting some environmental barriers to good communication.

Pigeon #1: Poor Lighting

Is your meeting room dreary and dark? If so, brighten it up. Add a couple of spotlights to the ceiling that shine at a forty-five degree angle toward the place where you usually stand to speak. Fluorescent lighting is cold and impersonal; add some warm incandescent lighting. I am convinced that if everyone in the room can see the sparkle in your eyes, your ability to communicate will take a huge leap forward.

As a professional entertainer, I have the privilege of performing in a multitude of environments. The two places in the world with the worst lighting are the two places that should have the best lighting: churches and hotel ballrooms. (Many times they also have atrocious sound, but more about that later.) The lights in many churches and ballrooms shine straight down from the ceiling. This kind of lighting effectively lights the hair; however, well-lighted hair is not essential to good communication.

If you can see the eyes of the speaker, you can see his or her heart. If you can see his or her heart, you can better hear his or her words. Eyeglasses tend to reflect light, so the audience can't see a speaker's eyes. When I heard that a well-known speech instructor counseled executives to remove their glasses when they made presentations, I thought, *Now that's carrying it a bit too far.* However, in our next Dynamic Communicators Workshop, I experimented with that suggestion. I asked my students to remove their glasses before their presentations. The results were astounding. The critique sheets abounded with comments such as, "Much better without the glasses," "It was great to see your eyes." If we believe the eyes are the window to the soul and that eye contact is of primary importance, then we should, if possible, speak without glasses.

Ensure that the lighting allows the listeners to see your eyes and face. Brighten the room. The meeting room doesn't have to look like a nightclub stage, but it should be bright and cheery. A rule of thumb is, if everyone in the room can see that little white reflection of light in your eyes, then the lighting is good.

Speakers often shoot themselves in the foot when it comes to lighting. A common mistake is for a speaker to stand in front of a brightly lighted window. God made the human eyes so they adjust to brightness. If you stand in front of a bright window facing a group, your facial features will be almost indistinguishable.

Try this experiment. Ask someone to stand in front of a brightly lighted background such as a window. Go to the back of the room and try to distinguish the details of his or her features. Your eyes quickly will adjust to the bright background and the person's features will be dark and indistinguishable. Only by great squinting effort can you see the face clearly. That effort can't be maintained for long.

Now place the person on the other side of the room so that the light illuminates his or her face. Have your back to the source of light. Now you are using light to make the facial features clear and easy to see—no need for squinting. If you ever speak to a group of kids whose faces are twisted into grotesque squinting positions, glance behind you.

I recently delivered a speech at an outdoor gathering. It was late in the afternoon and the sun was low on the horizon and at my back. This meant that 600 people were unable to look at me without risking blindness. How much better to have the sun at their back illuminating my features. Many churches don't have good lighting because a deacon or elder complained that the light was in their eyes when they were on the platform. That's the point. It is supposed to be in their eyes. If the lighting is right, it will be a little uncomfortable for the speaker. It is the audience, not the speaker, who must be comfortable and able to see.

Pigeon #2: The Wrong Room

Use a room that fits your group. Twelve teenagers huddled together at the front of a sanctuary that seats 500 is not an ideal setting for communication. It's even worse if the kids decide to spread out a little. Unless it's just impossible, find a place that will give your group a secure feeling.

It is always better to meet in a room that is too small than to meet in a large room and have a small group rattle about like peas in a pail. If you must meet in an overly large room, improvise to cut down the size. If an event involving fifty kids has just taken place in a gymnasium (the worst of all places to communicate), don't seat the kids on the bleachers to listen to your talk. The whole psychology of this arrangement works against you. A gym is usually a place of high energy and anticipation. When the place is full and a game is in progress, the reverberating sound and packed bleachers generate excitement. If you gather your little group together for a talk, the expectations in a place like this dominate. The lack of loud, excited voices creates an almost depressing atmosphere as your single, lonesome voice echoes off the walls the punch lines that you spoke three minutes before.

Why not plan fun and games at the gym since it was designed for that kind of activity? Then meet backstage or in a smaller room where a more intimate setting allows for maximum communication. If all of that fails, create your own space by speaking from a corner with the kids facing you. Remember three rules:

1. Even with large crowds, make the surroundings as warm and intimate as possible.
2. A full room is always better than an empty room. Two hundred kids who attend a meeting where ten have to stand in doorways will return home declaring that everybody was there. They will feel the successful dynamics of a full room. The same 200 will go home from the same meeting after being spread out in a 1,000-seat auditorium or sanctuary feeling that

not many people showed up. I would rather speak to 50 kids jammed in a small room than to 200 in an auditorium that will seat 1,000. The response is always better when the room is full. Make the room fit the crowd.

3. Always have something close behind you. A wall, a curtain, or a divider will do. Vast space behind a speaker is extremely distracting.

Pigeon #3: Interruptions and Distractions

Eliminate distractions. Whether they are pigeons sitting on the rafters, deacons walking in and out, or a loud air conditioner—distractions will short-circuit your attempts to communicate.

Arrange your room so that latecomers will arrive in the back; have someone assigned to quietly seat them (in the back). If your group is familiar with you, ask them to answer nature's call before or after your talk—not during your talk. Junior high kids seem to feel a meeting is not complete unless they leave with a group of their friends at least once.

If you meet in a home, make sure children and pets are caged during your talks. You may be good, but believe me, you can't compete with a puppy or a toddler. They will upstage you every time.

In many churches, halfway through the youth meeting or Sunday school class, a person (pigeon) interrupts the meeting (drops a pigeon missile) by coming into the room to collect the offering and to take attendance. I have been interrupted at least fifty times by this ritual. Is this an ancient church tradition? This pigeon needs to go. Collect the offering and take the attendance at the beginning of the class and leave the little envelope outside the door. The people who need this information and the dear folks who pick up the information for them have good intentions. Leave the information outside for them. You will make their job easier, and one more pigeon will be gone.

Pigeon #4: Room Temperature

This pigeon is so obvious, I will discuss it only briefly. If your meeting room is too hot, the reception of your speech will be cool. Remember that the bodies of fifty or sixty kids will raise the temperature of a room significantly. If the room is too cold, survival will be first on the listeners' minds; your speech will be second.

Your room is too cold if

- The kids are huddled close together in a corner of the room
- Small icicles are forming on the tips of the kids' noses
- There are any attempts to light a fire in the room

To keep the listeners' attention focused on you and your message, keep the room temperature comfortable.

The following are elements of your environment that will either help or hinder you. Use this list to check your situation, then give yourself a huge break by ridding yourself of any pigeons you might find.

1. Is the lighting bright and cheery? (Can the listeners see the sparkle in your eyes?)
2. What object or scene is behind you? (Is it distracting or depressing? Does a glaring window blind your audience?)
3. Does the room fit your group? (Remember: It's better to meet in a room too small than in a room too large.)
4. Is the arrangement of the room conducive to good communication? (Is it informal, with a minimum of distractions?)
5. Is the room temperature comfortable? (If the room is too hot, the reception will be cool.)

"MIKE": FRIEND OR FOE?

One of the greatest tools for effective communication is the modern microphone. It can enhance a good voice and cover flaws in a weak voice. It enables the communicator to whisper to an audience of 50 or 50,000. For the person who skillfully uses the microphone, it is his or her best friend. In the hands of a novice, it is an enemy—a roadblock to communication.

I've always been fascinated with sound systems, so I'm always surprised that many people fear the microphone. Many times while interviewing someone, I ask a question and then extend the microphone toward him in anticipation of an answer. Invariably the person recoils, as though I just thrust a burning torch toward his face.

There are several reasons why people fear the microphone. Some people are unaccustomed to hearing their own voices amplified. Others are afraid because the microphones must be held so close to the face to work correctly. The close proximity of this piece of metal violates our comfort zone. Still others feel a microphone gives too much of a "showbiz" atmosphere to a speech.

I have watched professional athletes, corporate executives, even movie personalities give addresses or make remarks standing three to five feet from the microphone, as though moving close might endanger them with electrocution. Men and women who are usually self-confident and articulate become tongue-tied and helpless when standing in front of a microphone.

All of these fears diminish with practice. After a while you will not even be aware of the microphone. And once you get used to its benefits, you will feel absolutely naked without it.

The microphone must be spoken into—not at—in order to work. These little marvels reproduce best at a distance of one to two inches from your lips. The microphone should be held just level with the bottom lip and at a forty-five-degree angle to the perpendicular plane of your face. If the microphone is held too high and too close to the face, the result will be an annoying popping sound whenever the letter "P" is pronounced. Too much bass also will produce this annoying sound. If you can stand in front of the microphone and repeat

"Peter Piper picked a peck of pickled peppers" without getting "pops" and "pows," you are holding it correctly.

Regardless of what you may have seen or heard, DO NOT give your talk with the mike touching your chin. Although this may be the optimum position for perfect sound, it looks stiff and is extremely distracting.

When you speak at various locations, arrive early enough to set the sound the way you like it. If you move much farther than six inches from most microphones, the resonance and quality of the sound begin to deteriorate. This means that if you plan to move about during your speech, you will need to remove the microphone from its stand and take it with you. This is the one disadvantage of a handheld microphone.

If you absolutely cannot overcome your discomfort with a microphone and a stand, then perhaps a lavaliere microphone would suit you better. A lavaliere attaches to your clothes and can be forgotten. Remember, however, if there is a cord, it cannot be forgotten. I will never forget the sight of a preacher in beautiful vestments lying on his back, legs and arms flailing wildly. He had tripped over his microphone cord. Needless to say, although I never will forget the incident, I can't begin to recall the topic or the purpose of his message.

If you use a cordless microphone (lavaliere or handheld), use only the best. The cheaper cordless mikes will pick up everything from stray radio stations to police cars. The last thing you need is to have your sound system blaring out the details of a drug bust in the middle of your speech. Don't laugh—it's happened.

I prefer the handheld microphone because of the flexibility of expression it allows. Held very close, it dramatizes a point. It can enhance every variation and voice inflection you wish to project. Held further away, it allows you to shout without breaking eardrums. A lavaliere gives a dependable but flat representation throughout your talk.

Almost all of my speeches are very physical. When I listen to recordings of my speeches made with a lavaliere, I notice that my movements cause a lot of distracting noises. However, there are many fine speakers who use a lavaliere, and you may wish to try one.

Another way to spot those who don't use a microphone correctly is to watch how they touch it. Every time you touch a microphone or stand, you draw attention to its presence. It is like having another person onstage distracting the audience as you speak. It may be stylish for a singer to coil the cord in his or her hand or to grasp the microphone with both hands. It may even be acceptable for a stand-up comedian to use the microphone as a prop. But unless you are singing or unless you are a stand-up comedian, leave the microphone alone. If you don't play with it, your audience will be unaware that it is there. Their attention will be focused on you and your message.

If you intend to hold the microphone during most of your talk, then move the stand out of your way. I prefer to take the microphone with me when I move and carefully replace it in the stand when I need both hands for gestures or need to read a passage from Scripture.

If you buy a sound system, choose one that is flexible and reproduces quality sound. I rarely like built-in systems; the speakers seem as though they always are broken. Many places have cheap speaker cans built into the ceiling. These systems produce a pinched, thin rattling sound that interferes with good communication. So many churches talk about a great God and marvelous grace over a sound system that makes it sound as though Mickey Mouse is delivering the message.

A portable system can be moved anywhere in the church (or in the world). A small pair of quality speakers and a powerful but compact amplifier are extremely portable; they will meet most any of your sound needs.

When other groups ask you to speak, be sure to indicate exactly what you require for sound and lights. I have learned the hard way to be very strict in my requirements. A high school principal asked me to address 1,500 students in an assembly. He warned me that the kids usually were rude during performances. I asked the principal to be sure there was a good sound system. He assured me they had a system that worked very well.

On the day of the program, fortunately, I came about a half hour early to check out the system. "The system" consisted of a portable tape recorder with about a two-inch speaker. The microphone cord was so short you couldn't speak without bending over. The resulting sound was like a rattlesnake with laryngitis. These people expected me to communicate with 1,500 hyper teenagers bending over and speaking into an unintelligible system. No wonder the kids were rude during performances! I refused to do the program without a decent system. It only took fifteen minutes for them to find and set up a system used by the music department. After the program, the "rude crowd" rewarded my efforts with a standing ovation. It was probably the first program in years they could hear.

Often the microphone is firmly planted in the middle of a podium. Get a microphone stand and get out from behind the pulpit or podium. For you, as a youth worker, huge pulpits or podiums serve no purpose other than to place a barrier between you and your audience. Some speakers get so used to hiding behind the podium that they are helpless without it. They don't know what to do with their hands and they feel very awkward. Learn to live without the podium. It is an eternal symbol of boredom to every teenager, and it is a freedom-restricting barrier to good communication. If you wish to communicate clearly, don't stand behind a big piece of wood. There should be nothing between you and your audience but words.

PART TWO
PRESENTATION:

Once
Your Lips
Start Moving

CHAPTER SIX

How to Talk Gooder

Beyond the basics, there are several aspects of communication that are rarely taught. Following are some secrets and some time-proven formulas that can only enhance your communication.

READING YOUR AUDIENCE:
TO WHOM DO YOU THINK YOU'RE TALKING?

One of the most impressive, creative, short-subject films I ever saw was titled *Lost Cause*. The camera framed a close-up of a very dramatic presentation given by an excellent speaker. He spoke of life-and-death issues, and he fervently called his audience to action. As he continued this persuasive oratory, the camera pulled back to reveal the beautiful platform from which he spoke. It was draped with flags and banners carrying the same message he was verbalizing. Then, in a quick move, the camera panned back to reveal an empty auditorium. The speaker was delivering his speech to 2,000 empty seats. It was indeed a lost cause.

The audience is the other half of the team. When a speaker approaches the stage without considering the audience, he or she may as well address an empty auditorium. From the beginning formation of a talk to the choice of illustrations and style of delivery, the successful speaker thinks of the audience.

The convention or retreat speaker who presents a canned speech, oblivious to the needs of the group, misses an

opportunity to meet kids right where they live. If there has been a tragedy in your church, it is best to forgo the usual "lesson" and speak to the needs of your audience. You can always pick up the lesson where you left off, but the teachable moment that is dictated by the immediate needs of your audience may be gone forever by tomorrow.

In the middle of one of my talks, some kids asked questions that indicated an immediate need that had to be met. At the time, I ignored the questions and bulled forward with "my talk." After the meeting I learned that the brother of one of the kids had been killed. My group desperately needed me to address the questions that this tragedy had elicited.

Sometimes we can be effective by rearranging our speech strategy midstride. There is nothing sacred about the talk we have prepared. If it doesn't meet a real need in the kids' lives, then it is a waste of time. During a talk, a speaker should also take note of nonverbal communication from the audience. This communication takes many forms: The kids may exhibit boredom with a universal yawn, or they may show extreme restlessness. Sometimes it's worth the effort to stop talking and find out what's causing that restlessness.

I've had a whole audience mentally leave me because a young man was standing at the window making faces. I didn't know what was causing the disturbance; all I knew was that nobody's attention was focused on me. Had I continued with my speech it would've been an exercise in futility.

I asked the audience what the disturbance was. When they told me, I simply walked over to the edge of the window and peeked out with one eye. When the intruder saw the one eye staring directly at him, he quickly left! The kids laughed, I laughed, and I once again had their rapt attention. Somewhere, there's a young man telling a story of a Sunday school class with a very strange teacher!

An audience is a collection of people; they collectively express their attitudes and feelings. Learn to read your audience by watching their expressions and adjusting to their attitudes.

THE FIRST FIFTY WORDS:
WAS IT SOMETHING I SAID?

What will make the audience pay attention? At the beginning of your talk there occurs a rare opportunity that may not present itself in quite the same way at any other time. In those first few seconds you have an attentive audience. And in those first few seconds that audience decides whether or not you are worth listening to. Those first fifty words are the most important words you will speak.

Speakers who often talk to groups other than their own should develop three or four openings that are proven attention-getters. These openings can be a story, joke, an astounding truth, unique visual demonstration, or a short, startling reading, statement, or question.

The opening doesn't necessarily have to relate directly to the objective of your speech, although it is more powerful if it does. The opening should set you up, not place barriers between you and your audience. I once saw a man step to the front, draw a gun from his coat, and fire it at his audience. Of course, it was loaded with blanks, and it did get the kids' attention. However, they never recovered from the shock and did not hear his message, which was totally unrelated to the illustration. Even though the speaker succeeded in getting the kids out from under their chairs and back in their seats, they still wouldn't calm down.

A very dear friend of mine from Canada is a superb communicator. He stood in front of about 300 young people from his group and began a weeklong camp in Florida. Anticipation was high. He began by announcing that a mental patient had escaped from a nearby institution and had been seen in the same complex they were staying in. This person had allegedly attacked some of the girls in the group, and everyone was to be on the lookout. My friend explained that one of the girls who was attacked had stabbed the madman with a pencil. She had driven the pencil right through his hand. My friend told the kids that if they met any strangers they should glance at the hands to check for a wound. The audience was dead silent.

At this point, my friend took his hand from his pocket and began to casually make other announcements. His hand was heavily bandaged with a spot of red in the center. It was all a joke, but it backfired terribly. Many of his own young people were so angry they refused to speak to him. His heart was broken as he spent most of the week trying to regain their confidence.

In this case, the first fifty words destroyed several days of ministry. When chosen carefully and prayerfully, introductory words can be the launching pad of dynamic speech and ministry. Never start the adrenaline flowing in a group of teenagers unless you're prepared to handle it. In other words, unless your church has its own SWAT team, forget it.

If you lead a youth group or teach a Sunday school class, your group should always look with anticipation toward your opening. You must prepare a new and unique opening for each talk. Nonverbal openings can be very effective. A slide on a screen showing a starving child and the caption "Who cares?" would set the stage for a talk on our responsibility as Christians to those in need. Keep in mind that your first fifty words are important, regardless of the visual aides you use.

Ken Overstreet, a great youth communicator from San Diego, used an opening illustration that never failed to have the audience hanging on every word. He described in detail an experience he had riding in the cockpit of a U.S. Air Force fighter plane. Every observation and sensation was described so clearly, I could feel myself sitting in the cockpit with him. When he described the beat of his heart in anticipation of the flight, my heart began to race as though I were there too.

Ken had paid careful attention during the pilot's briefing. He recounted to us in detail how pulling a red and yellow handle would explosively eject his seat into the atmosphere in an emergency. He stressed the importance of counting to ten and then firmly pulling the rip cord to open the parachute.

My heart raced as he relived the powerful force he felt upon takeoff and the exhilaration of maneuvers that left him weightless. Then he retold how the pilot discovered a fire in the left engine and ejected them both from the cockpit. I gasped. At this point, we pictured Ken reaching down—his body frozen in the now silent sky. Ken said, "For a moment I groped for the rip cord ring. I had no sensation of falling, I just felt an incredible rush of wind and paralyzing fear.

"My fingers found the ring. I pulled the cord. Nothing happened. I pulled again. The cord wouldn't budge! I could see the earth coming toward me. With a mighty heave of all my strength, I pulled. A scream tore from my throat as I woke up sitting in bed, jerking frantically on the cord of my pajama bottoms."

It had all been a dream! But Ken's skill as a communicator had made it my dream too, and as he moved into his talk on fear, we were like putty in his hands.

Maybe your openings won't be as dramatic as any of those I've mentioned. But variety is essential when you speak to the same group of kids week after week. An opening that is almost always effective begins like this: "Close your eyes. Clear your mind." (Give the audience a moment to do so.) "Now imagine . . ." Then take your audience with you to imagine any situation. This also is an excellent discussion starter. Be creative here. Spend quality time preparing an opening that will grab the attention of your audience and lead you toward your objective. Don't allow familiarity to breed sloppiness.

I've lost count of the times I've seen youth leaders begin their talks by saying, "Okay, let's settle down." Now there is an opening sure to gain you three or four seconds of rapt attention. On the other hand, if you take the time to make your beginnings fascinating and varied, you will find your audience waits with anticipation to hear what you have to say.

"Last night I awoke with a start as I heard my wife's frantic whisper, 'Listen, someone is in the house!' It took only seconds to become fully alert when I heard the unmistakable

sound of stealthy footsteps. I quietly slipped from bed and reached for the hall light. I was prepared to defend my life and home but felt pretty helpless as I stood shaking in my underwear. I turned on the light."

I bet you'd like to hear the rest of this true story. Too bad. It was just an illustration of how those first words can make you pay attention. I will tell you that no one was in the house, and one scruffy cat that had fallen into the clothes hamper spent a cold night outside. I'll also tell you that next time I'm going to slip on a pair of trousers before I yell, "Who's there?"

ESTABLISHING RAPPORT:
THEY LOVE ME, THEY LOVE ME NOT

Those first words of your speech should not only get the attention of your audience, they should be the first step in establishing rapport. One could get the attention of his or her group by stepping to the front naked; however, I doubt this method would establish rapport. The youth speaker who shot a gun at his audience got their attention, but at the price of erecting a barrier between him and his audience.

Look at how one youth leader used the anxiety caused by a gun to teach a valuable lesson. One Sunday morning she announced to her group she had a witnessing tool that always caught the full attention of the person with whom she was sharing her faith. "Are you tired of your friends laughing in your face when you try to share the message of Christ's love?" she asked with evangelistic fervor.

"Yes!" her audience yelled—which indicated she already had established rapport.

"Would you like to have access to a communication tool that will make your friends want to listen?"

"Yes!" they yelled.

"Well, I have discovered a method that works every time." She opened a box and carefully displayed none other than a .357 Magnum, exhorting the audience never to leave home without it. There was some laughter and some expressions of

anxiety. When the laughter died, she looked those kids straight in the eyes and said, "You know, a lot of times our insensitive approach to witnessing is about as offensive as holding a gun to the person with whom we are trying to share. When we throw tracts and canned speeches at people without taking the time to really care, we make them feel like the victims of a drive-by shooting."

She had the kids' attention, and she didn't have to shoot the gun to shock them. She didn't even have to touch it. This illustration led right into her topic, and they were ready to listen.

Other factors that establish rapport between a speaker and his or her audience are a sense of self-confidence and personal vulnerability. Confidence comes from being well-prepared and believing in your message. It also comes from a lack of fear of being in front of an audience. That lack of fear is demonstrated both verbally and nonverbally.

- Verbal signs: your command of the language, your choice of words, your use of effective illustrations, and your clear presentation of the speech's objective (without groping for words). If you are confident, it will show in the smooth flow of your delivery.
- Nonverbal signs: good eye contact, powerful gestures, and an aggressive stance.

Confidence causes your audience to believe you have something worthwhile to say. Because you are relaxed, they are relaxed.

The vulnerability that builds audience rapport is more difficult to describe. It is more an attitude than a technique. Personal vulnerability from the stage is communicated by a caring sensitivity toward the audience. It is the touch of informality that makes members of the audience believe you are communicating with them, not delivering a canned speech at them. Personal vulnerability is also communicated by an openness in your presentation that allows the audience to see that you are human. Illustrations from your personal life and revelations of some of your feelings and weaknesses allow the audience to identify with you.

A young man in California stood in front of one of my communication classes to deliver his second speech. After an excellent beginning, he faltered. Unflustered, he said, "Excuse me, I was so absorbed in listening to the speeches before mine that I have momentarily lost my place." His statement was made with the confidence of someone who was simply telling the truth. Then he asked me if he might start over so his speech wouldn't contain this flaw. I refused to let him start over.

His vulnerability and confidence in handling the situation had turned a weakness into a strength. All students in the audience noted it in their critiques. He had told a room of nervous people, just like himself, that they had absorbed him in their speeches. They not only understood, they were flattered. They also identified with his predicament and felt no discomfort or nervousness because of his excellent handling of the situation. I told this young man that if he ever became eloquent but lost his sense of appropriate vulnerability (that had so captured his audience's attention), he would have lost a great asset.

Some books suggest that the speaker must remain aloof from the audience. I disagree. I don't suggest speakers apologize to the audience, debasing themselves, telling the audience they are frightened or admitting they are ill-prepared. But instead, speakers should actively pursue the ability to remain human to the audience. If the kids we speak to react by saying, "I could never be like that," if they stand in awe of us as aloof untouchable heroes, then our messages will be perceived in the same light. Kids will believe their hero youth director might be capable of living up to the challenge of his or her own message, but these same challenges will seem out of reach for them. We must allow our communication and our lives to be vulnerable. Then our listeners will identify with and more realistically perceive our message.

It is significant to see Christ's example in this regard. In order to deliver the most important message ever needed by humanity, Christ became one of us, lived among us, and felt our pain.

- "For we do not have a high priest who is unable to sympathize with our weaknesses, but we have one who has been tempted in every way, just as we are—yet was without sin" (Hebrews 4:15).
- "[Christ] made himself nothing, taking the very nature of a servant, being made in human likeness" (Philippians 2:7).

In every way, Christ exhibited the true principles of a good communicator. His message was heard and continues to change the lives of those who respond to it.

A SECRET FORMULA FOR RESULTS: BUILD TENSION AND KEEP IT

One of the key formulas for gaining and keeping the interest of your audience is this: Reveal your objective in such a way as to leave the audience with questions. Then build your talk so that when you conclude, you have answered those questions. Kids want to know what you're going to talk about. No one likes to be kept guessing. Think of it this way: Chances are remote that kids are going to sit on the edge of their seats trying to figure out the purpose of your speech. If you tell them the purpose (or objective) of your speech near the beginning, it's out in the open. But you build tension as to how you are going to accomplish that objective. If you say to an audience, "Tonight I am going to show you how you can make new friends in one day," the audience begins to wonder, "How can I make new friends in one day?" They should want to hear the answer. If you continue with, "There are three actions you can take that will guarantee you a new friend by tomorrow," your audience should want to hear what those three actions are. If at any place in your speech you give such general or exhaustive information that it breaks the tension, then you are going to lose your audience. For example, if you introduce your objective by saying you should love your neighbor because the Bible says so, then you leave yourself with nothing else to say. The tension is broken; there are no more questions to be asked. You might as well fold up your notes and go home. The better way to introduce this talk would be to add that all-important "key word" we talked about in chapter 2. "Tonight I would like to encourage you to love your neighbor for three reasons." The question "What reasons?" immediately comes to mind. The tension is intact, and answering those questions becomes the framework for your speech. Now those clever illustrations will have more meaning, and your speech will be more powerful. Illustrations that would otherwise seem weak or meaningless take on meaning when the audience knows what you are trying to accomplish and is looking for answers you have promised. Once they know your purpose, they will make the connections between the separate parts of your talk before you explain it verbally. Read the following illustration:

> In college I was asked to prepare a lesson to teach to my speech class. We were graded on our creativity and ability to drive home a point in a memorable way. The title of my talk was, "The Law of the Pendulum and Belief." After I told the class that I intended to reveal the law of true belief, I spent twenty minutes carefully teaching the physical principle that governs a swinging pendulum. I could see the look of puzzlement on their faces. What did the law of the pendulum have to do with belief? The tension built as I proceeded. I kept reminding them of my objective along the way. That way they would know I was still headed in the right direction and continue to wonder how all of this would come together.
>
> The law of the pendulum is this: A pendulum can never return to a point higher than the point from which it was released. Because of friction and gravity, when the pendulum returns, it will fall short of its original release point. Each time it swings it makes less and less of an arc, until finally it is at rest. This point of rest is called the state of equilibrium, where all forces acting on the pendulum are equal.
>
> I attached a three-foot string to a child's toy top and secured it to the top of the blackboard with a thumbtack.

I pulled the top to one side and made a mark on the blackboard where I let it go. Each time it swung back I made a new mark. It took less than a minute for my little pendulum to complete its swinging and come to rest. When I finished the demonstration, the markings on the blackboard proved my thesis.

I then asked how many people in the room believed the law of the pendulum was true. All of my classmates raised their hands, and so did the teacher. Thinking my presentation was over, he started to walk to the front of the room. In reality it had just begun. Hanging from the steel ceiling beams in the middle of the room was a large, crude but functional pendulum (250 pounds of metal weights tied to four strands of 500-pound-test parachute cord).

I invited the instructor to climb up on a table and sit in a chair with the back of his head against a cement wall. Then I slowly brought the 250 pounds of metal up to his nose. Holding the huge pendulum just a fraction of an inch from his face, I once again explained the law of the pendulum he had applauded only moments before, and I said, "If the law of the pendulum is true, then when I release this mass of metal, it will swing across the room and return short of the release point. Your nose will be in no danger."

After that final restatement of this law, I looked him in the eye and asked, "Sir, do you believe this law is true?"

There was a long pause. Huge beads of sweat formed on his upper lip and then he nodded weakly and whispered, "Yes." I could see looks of understanding begin to appear in the audience. The connection between the objective of the talk and this illustration was beginning to come together.

I released the pendulum. It made a swishing sound as it arced across the room. At the far end of its swing, it paused momentarily and started back. I never saw a man move so fast in my life. He literally dived from the table. Deftly stepping around the still-swinging pendulum, I asked the class, "Does he believe the law of the pendulum?"

The students answered unanimously, "NO!"

If I were to ask you the purpose of this illustration, some of you would know. But none of you would have known until the very end of the illustration. The objective of my talk that night was, "What you believe is evidenced by how you live, not by what you say." Specifically, the two actions that allow you to determine true belief are (1) don't listen to what people say and (2) watch how they act.

About halfway through my talk, the audience began to see the real significance of this illustration. Before the illustration was over, they could see what I was trying to communicate. Because I stated my objective, the audience members became more than passive observers waiting for me to tell them the significance of the story. Instead, they actively participated in tying the story to the purpose of the speech. A conclusion reached by a member of your audience as a result of logical reasoning will be retained much longer than any conclusion you draw for your audience.

Give your audience a sense of direction. Build tension that demands answers. Give them an opportunity to make sense of your talk. Then clearly and logically, using the SCORRE method, satisfy the need you have built. Finally, summarize in a brief and powerful way the truth you have tried to communicate.

FINISH ON TIME, FINISH ON TARGET: IT'S ONLY A MATTER OF TIME

One of the greatest disciplines for effective communication is to finish on time. Going over the time allotted for your talk rarely is an indication that the audience demanded to hear more. It is most often an indication that the speaker was not prepared. Your audience will be more comfortable if they know the time frame of your message.

Your effectiveness decreases in direct proportion to the number of minutes you go over your allotted time limit. Teenagers are particularly sensitive to time. No matter how fantastic your communication may be, your message will be

lost if the kids' minds are on pizza or if their parents are waiting because you were insensitive to the time.

Make the time limit a part of your planning. If you are asked to speak at an event, keep your speech within the allotted time limit. (Your welcome in the future will depend on respecting this rule.) If you are leading a study or speaking to your church group, determine limits by keeping your speech specific, short, and no more than twenty minutes. If you can't say what you want to say in twenty minutes, one of two things is true: Either you don't know what you are talking about (ready to ramble) or you are trying to say too much. Divide the rest of your time among creative use of videos, discussion, films, audiotapes, and so forth (see chapter 9). Stick religiously to those parameters and you will develop a growing ability to say what you want to say within any time frame allowed.

One Sunday, after keeping a combination of youth and adults in total rapt attention for nearly an hour, I stood in the back of the church expecting the usual compliments on a fine message. But the compliments were few; even the traditional handshakes were sparse. The occasional teenager who had time to stop was quickly hurried out by a scowling parent. What had I said? Had I violated a tradition? Was my theology in question? My confusion was quickly answered by a sweet elderly lady who stopped and said, "Young man [I was young at the time], whatever plans you have for lunch, I would like you to cancel them. I would like you to join me and my family this noon for burnt roast."

There was nothing wrong with my theology or delivery. Instead, I had violated a rule very important to effective communication: Finish on time. Breaking that rule caused a number of people to stop thinking about the topic of my sermon and start thinking about burnt roasts and ruined schedules.

Just as important as finishing on time is another rule: Finish on target. How many times have you listened to a speaker wrap up a nice talk and then continue on with another point? Long ago I lost track of the times I observed a perfectly fine talk ruined because the speaker didn't know how (or when) to end. If the opening of your speech is of prime importance, then the ending is a close second. The last words you say are the last words your audience hears. They are the part of your speech they will remember the longest. Your closing should include an excellent illustration or an attention-getting point, and it should summarize the objective of your speech.

When you approach this dynamic and life-changing close, it is acceptable and even wise to tell your audience you are about finished. Words like "In closing" or "I'd like to wrap this up by ..." will stop the kids from looking at their watches or thinking about their parents waiting in the parking lot. By all means tell the listeners you are finishing and then finish. The words "in conclusion" were never meant to be the title of another twenty-minute sermon. If you tell them you are finishing and don't finish, believe me, you are finished anyway. The next time you speak to an audience and tell them to pay attention because you are almost finished, they won't believe you.

One additional note: When you pray, pray. Prayer is not meant to be a time for including the points you missed in your sermon. Nor is it the time for another sermon. It's not even a time for summary. Prayer is prayer. Keep your prayers after a talk short and to the point, thanking God for what he is going to do, asking his Spirit to move kids to action, or asking God to use what you have said. Both God and the kids heard the message. This is not the time to give it again.

AIMING FOR ACTION:
AVOID THE LOCKER-ROOM PILEUP

If your communication with youth is simply a form of entertainment or a baby-sitting time killer, then this book has been for naught. If our words have no purpose, then the work required to become the best we can be is an exercise in futility.

Truly effective communication always brings results. Therefore, one of our goals as good communicators is to know the results we are trying to achieve. An often forgotten aspect of communication is that which should take place after our talk is over. We must not become spiritual teases, challenging our teenagers to a lifestyle or a commitment we are not willing to help them accomplish.

Bill Cosby tells the story of a football team that was losing miserably at halftime. The score was 58–0. If there was any hope of pulling this game out of the hole, the coach would have to do some major motivating in the locker room. He gathered his battered, frustrated team at one end of the steaming room. He questioned their manhood, he criticized their performance, and he challenged them to give their all in the second half.

A spark of excitement began to grow in the room as he allowed them a glimpse of the glory that would be theirs if they came from behind and won this game. The spark grew to a roaring flame as he had them chanting "Win! Win! Win!" There was no doubt in any of the players' minds that they could do it. As the chant changed to "Kill! Kill! Kill!" the coach screamed, "Now go get 'em!" and they rushed for the door. The locker-room door was locked.

After only a few moments of trying to break it down, the team sat in a sweaty, discouraged heap. They had been motivated to accomplish a great task, but because of the locked door, there was no opportunity to accomplish that task.

If we challenge our group members to a discipleship commitment, our communication is not complete until we unlock opportunities for them to apply such commitment. If we are speaking to kids about sexual responsibility in dating, then it's essential we offer them counseling and classes to help achieve those goals. If we challenge our kids to help the less fortunate, then why not provide an opportunity to paint a house, clean a yard, or visit a rest home? When we invite kids to trust Christ, it is imperative we give them an opportunity to do so. When we close our talk in prayer and make our concluding remarks, in many aspects our communication has just begun. Now it is of utmost importance to provide experiences to help our youth respond to the challenge we have given them.

CHAPTER SEVEN

Let Your Body Talk

Nowhere in Scripture can we find support for the idea that the lips are the only part of the body that should move during a speech, yet this idea came from somewhere. It's time we give our eyes, hands, bodies, lips, and voices the chance to work together as a team. Even if people listen to us just to see what will move next, at least they will listen.

EYE CONTACT:
LOOK AT ME WHEN I'M TALKING TO YOU

The speaker's greatest tools, other than the lips, are the eyes. The old saying that the eyes are a gateway through which we can glimpse a person's soul is true. When requiring the absolute truth from one of my children, I will demand, "Look at me when I'm talking to you." By looking into my kids' eyes, I can see the truth. When they are sick or disheartened, the first place it shows is in their eyes.

I have watched two teenagers communicate undying love across a room without saying a word. In just the briefest glance they set the room on fire with their passion. I also have observed a disobedient child stopped in his tracks by a warning glance from a mother or father. "If looks could kill," my mother used to tell my sister after she had sent daggers my way with her eyes, "your brother would be lying dead on the floor right now."

Simple recall of our experience teaches that the eyes are indeed a window to the soul. Regarding this truth about our eyes, we must follow two rules for good communication.

Rule #1: Your audience must be able to see your eyes. As we discussed in chapter 5, this rule is absolutely essential. The next time you are to speak, ask someone to stand where you will make your presentation. Can you see that person's eyes clearly? Is a sparkle of light reflected from the eyes? If so, your eyes will enhance your communication. If your eyes are hidden by shadows and the lighting is dull, you will begin your speech with two strikes against you.

Rule #2: You must look at their eyes. Establishing eye contact is one of the most important factors of good communication. I have never been able to trust anyone who can't look me in the eyes as he or she talks. The man who tries to sell me a car and will not look me in the eye as he speaks will never get my business. His reluctance to look at me communicates that he's hiding something or that he's ashamed or, even worse, that he's lying to me.

In twenty years of observing some of the finest communicators in the world, I have found that all of them establish excellent eye contact as they speak. Eye contact tells your audience that you are confident and that you believe in what you are saying. Eye contact tells your audience that you are speaking directly to them and you want them to hear your message. If your eyes are darting around the room or if you speak to some imaginary point above their heads, your kids will hear you preach at them, not communicate with them. Nobody likes to be preached at, yet almost everyone enjoys being communicated with.

When conversing with a friend, good eye contact is easy to identify—you look into his or her eyes. The same is true when speaking to an audience. Eye contact is most effective when you pick out individual people and speak directly to them. Complete several sentences while looking directly into their eyes. Then pick a new person and speak directly to him or her for a while.

If a conscious effort to establish and hold individual eye contact makes you uncomfortable, then you probably have been scanning your audience or speaking around them. A scanner's eyes never stay in one place for more than a second. Some scanners seem to focus on nothing in particular, but move their eyes continuously back and forth across the audience. It's almost as though the eyes are out of focus. On videotape this stands out clearly.

Other scanners hesitate only momentarily to look at many different individuals in the room. Eye contact is established only for a second. Then almost out of fear, the eyes move on. Sometimes the scanning falls into a rhythmic pattern, where the head swings back and forth like swaying children singing a nursery rhyme.

I have observed entire speeches in which the speaker never even glanced at anyone in the audience. These people looked at doors, windows, ceilings, and even at traffic going by outside. To an audience, a speaker like this appears nervous and ill at ease. This kind of speaker will find it very difficult to hold teenagers' attention.

If you find that you are a scanner, please believe that you will triple your effectiveness as a speaker by consciously making every effort to establish eye contact. Videotape every message you deliver. Position the video camera somewhere in the audience where a person would usually sit and at about the same height. Before you begin your talk, pick several people in the group to look at when you deliver your speech. Pretend the camera is one of those people. As you deliver your talk, look directly into the lens while emphasizing some of your main points. (Keep at it—this is not easy.) Make sure you deliver several sentences before you move on to another person. Then repeat the same process. Later, when you watch this tape, you will know immediately whether your eye contact needs improvement. You will see yourself exactly as the person sitting in that spot would have seen you. You will notice how uncomfortable it is to see the speaker's eyes flicker away from yours rather than speak directly to you with confidence. You will also see the power of that moment you looked into the lens. This will be a historic moment. You will establish eye contact with yourself. You may even be moved to respond to your own message.

If you begin to establish good eye contact, you will occasionally find that some people in your audience cannot meet your gaze. When they see you talking directly to them, they look away or avert their eyes downward. This isn't bad. Speak to them a moment longer, even though they aren't looking. If they look up, smile and reassure them with your eyes. If after a moment they don't look up, move on. Don't be intimidated by this phenomenon. Kids are listening. Eventually a group of young people you speak to often will become more comfortable with your talking to them instead of at them.

I once observed a youth leader give an entire speech while watching a spider make its way slowly across a beam in the ceiling. The speaker's eyes never left the spider as his voice droned on. I'll bet you can guess what every eye in the audience was focused on. That's right—on the spider. I don't remember what he talked about, but I do remember one important thing: The spider was gray and black and it was missing one leg.

Eye contact can be overdone if you stare at one person incessantly, but this is rare. Even when speaking to 5,000 people, none of whom I can see because of a glaring spotlight, I pick out a spot in the darkness where I know people are sitting and speak to the person I imagine sitting there. Then I pick another spot and continue. The kids sitting in the audience don't know I can't see them. Often they will come up after a program and say, "Remember me? I was the one you pointed to when you asked the question about parents."

In one of my comedy routines I deliberately want someone in the audience to hesitate when I ask for his or her name. This is accomplished by looking intently into the audience but into no one's eyes. I generally pick a spot toward the back of the audience between two people. I look at that spot and ask,

"What is your name?" Invariably several people in the area look around to see to whom I am speaking. The kids don't respond, because they don't feel I am speaking to them. This is because I am not looking directly into a specific person's eyes. When I do look directly into someone's eyes way back in the audience and ask, "What is your name?" many times three or four people answer at once or ask, "Who, me?"

The point is crystal clear. In a large audience, if you don't look at one specific person, no one will feel you are talking to him or her. If you look directly into someone's eyes, the person knows you are talking to him or her, and several people nearby think the same thing. Eye contact is a key ingredient of good communication.

GESTURES: ARE YOU A FLIPPER, A FLAPPER, OR A FANTASY MERCHANT?

Just as artists use paintbrushes, speakers use gestures to add color and detail to every verbal picture they try to create. We never realize how important gestures are until we try to communicate without them. When gestures are used effectively, they enhance communication; used improperly, gestures serve as distractions.

It is difficult to demonstrate the effective use of gestures within the limits of the printed word. Once again, viewing a video of yourself and consciously watching your gestures is the most effective way to see whether your body is helping or hindering your communication. Following are some simple guidelines for improving your gestures.

1. Don't be a flipper. Flippers are people who restrain gestures. Rather than actually producing a genuine gesture, they flip their wrists in halfhearted attempts. Evidently, this is to show the audience that they were thinking of a very demonstrative, grown-up gesture but didn't know how to follow through with it. Wrist-flipper motions are sometimes practiced with the hands hanging at the sides. More often you

see flippers practice this art with the elbows bent and the hands fairly close together at about waist level. In this position, the hands are often flipped together. Done from any position, flipping gestures are always distracting. Dolphins have flippers. Let them do the flipping. People were made to gesture.

2. Don't be a flapper. The opposite of flippers are flappers. These speakers demonstrate their points and emotions with uncontrolled, wild throwing motions of the arms. When the flapper really gets going, the audience sits on the edge of their seats in great anticipation, waiting for the speaker to become airborne. The unfortunate truth is that flappers provide so much entertainment with their arms that the message of the speech is often lost.

3. Be a fantasy merchant. These people have developed the ability to paint with their hands, body, and face a picture illustrative of their message. They effectively use gestures to take you beyond words to the place of which they speak. They make you feel the emotions they are feeling.

To be a fantasy merchant, practice your gestures in front of a mirror. This will help you spot mistakes that detract from your speech. Ask a few people to watch you speak and evaluate your flipping, flapping, flying, and swaying.

Practice until gestures come naturally to you and appear natural to your audience. Keep in mind that your arms do not need to move all the time. Just as it is acceptable to have moments of silence in a speech, it is also fine to deliver parts of your speech with your hands resting comfortably at your sides. Once you have mastered the art of natural gesturing and you no longer feel self-conscious about your arms, you will find that you won't have to practice gestures. They will become a spontaneous and natural part of your communication.

Gestures should help you communicate details that can't be communicated any other way. The sentence "The man was the size of a small boy" can only be fully demonstrated by showing how small the man was.

Gestures also serve as exclamation points. Saying "When the mirror broke, my heart almost stopped," while clutching your heart, gives the words a sense of drama that can only emphasize the point and help the audience understand the emotion of the moment.

Practice, relax, be natural. Effective use of gestures is an important part of speaking.

FACIAL AND BODY EXPRESSIONS: LOOK, MARTHA! HER EYEBROWS MOVED!

Facial expression is a tremendous tool to enhance your talks. A raised eyebrow, a momentary wide-eyed look of surprise, an expression of intense concentration—these are examples of facial expressions that give personal feeling to your message. Every person reading this book has heard a politician, teacher, or preacher give a dry, boring speech. You may even have leaned over to a friend and asked, "Why doesn't he put some life into it?" Few things bring life to a speech more than a face that shows all the expressions of a real, live person.

One of the reasons so many political speeches seem boring is because they are. They are often read, so there is little opportunity for expression. You don't need to clown around or overdo it. Just give your face a chance to show what you feel.

Mike Warnke wrinkles his entire face into a scowl as he tells of how tired he is of Christians walking around with such frowns. "I've been a Christian for fifty years," he growls. "It's wonderful." Changing his expression, he continues, "If it's so wonderful, tell your face. It's obvious your face doesn't know how wonderful it is." My advice to you is the same: Whatever you try to say, tell your face so that your face can express what you feel in your heart. Your facial expressions give life to your talk.

Practice facial expressions by videotaping a close-up of your face. Record a speech and watch yourself. If you were in

the audience, would you agree with the person's message? Does the face express feelings about the speech's content?

You also can practice facial expressions by mirroring with a friend. Have your friend ask you to express concern, sorrow, enthusiasm, excitement, fear, joy, puzzlement, and so forth. Critique each other. Don't become mime artists and overact. Learn to let your expressions come freely and naturally.

Body stance also speaks volumes. The stand you take as you deliver your speech is like one big gesture. Your posture can help you communicate confidence and help you command the attention of your audience.

As a general rule for maximum effect, the speaker's posture should be an aggressive one. Stand erect with your shoulders back and one foot slightly in front of the other. Lean slightly toward your audience. If it is true that your body is one big gesture, then occasionally use your whole body as a gesture. If you say, "I was so disheartened I couldn't face another day," and allow your shoulders to slump and your head to hang slightly, you make your audience feel what you are describing.

Say these words one at a time—out loud: "I was proud." Now stand in front of a mirror. Stand a moment and say these words again, slowly and emphatically: "I! Was! Proud!" Notice the difference? Close your fist and repeat the sentence. You just used all the means discussed in this section to enhance the meaning of three words. See what a difference it makes? You even feel proud, don't you?

VOICE: YOUR VOICE CAN GET IN THE WAY

There are five elements of a voice that we rarely consider in our speaking. We sometimes pay little attention to or neglect these aspects because we feel that nothing can be done to improve them. You can improve your voice by working on the following five elements.

Volume: Your Volume Speaks Volumes

This element of your voice has a tremendous effect on kids' willingness to listen. Errors in volume are most often made by those who speak too softly. The comprehension and retention of our message will be questionable if we force the audience to work to hear what we're saying. If you have been around kids very long, you already know that most teenagers don't like work. They will not expend a great deal of energy to catch every word you say. Instead they will start conversations of their own or find other distractions.

If your voice is naturally soft, then by all means use a microphone. If you speak frequently and in a variety of settings, strengthen your voice by taking voice lessons. Singers and actors do this all the time. If you want your message to be heard, you must be heard! Any effort to help strengthen your voice will be well rewarded.

Less frequently we encounter speakers who talk too loudly. These people tend to slightly irritate their audience. Remember, kids are at an age when they resist unreasonable authority. In fact, they often resist authority—period. The "drill sergeant's" delivery will create a level of conscious and unconscious irritation in the group.

The other problem with the screaming-eagle speaker is that he or she allows no room for flexibility of expression. If you are speaking very loudly through your speech, how do you vary your voice to emphasize a point?

If the reason you speak loudly is because of the size of your group, use a sound system, and let it do the work while you concentrate on communicating. But be careful here, too. A while ago I squirmed for forty-five minutes while a speaker yelled through a sound system at 2,000 teenagers. Everyone in the room could have heard him deliver his talk in a normal voice. He not only blew out the speaker, he blew his chances of effectively communicating with these kids. About a fourth of the way through his talk, my body and mind were fatigued from listening to him scream. Just last month I received a letter from a teenage friend who had attended a large youth gathering in Orlando. I will give you her direct quote without revealing the speaker's name. She wrote, "Most of the sessions were good but I didn't like [the speaker]. He yells a lot and seems to be mad all the time!" I'm sure this speaker thought he was being powerful when, in reality, he was overpowering. The rule on volume is, learn to project, but speak in a normal voice; give yourself tremendous leeway to use whispers or shouts when they are needed.

Pitch: Too High or Too Low and the Batter May Walk

I know of nothing more irritating than a high-pitched, squeaking speech. Whether it's the taste of our culture or simply the design of our eardrums, a whiny or high-pitched delivery alienates any audience—especially a young one. Generally people who speak too loudly also have a tendency to raise the pitch of their voice to an irritating level. Women, because of their naturally high pitch, can really have a problem here.

If you are uncertain of the quality of your voice, record yourself speaking, and then listen to the tape. If you find yourself wincing and feeling uncomfortable, you'll know you have a problem with pitch. Contact a voice instructor and ask for exercises to help lower your pitch. These exercises usually involve speaking vowel sounds in a low voice for a period of time each day and disciplining yourself to speak more softly, which will usually mean speaking lower.

Once again, a sound system can be your salvation. If the only way you can lower the pitch of your voice is to speak more softly than can be heard easily, use a sound system. You will be amazed at the change that can take place in your speaking voice over a relatively short period of time.

I remember clearly the first time I heard my voice on tape; I winced through the whole experience. After about a week of exercises I could hear a difference. A month of conscious effort resulted in a significantly more pleasant voice to listen to. If you are serious about being an excellent communicator, start working on that pitch now.

Resonance: At the Tone, the Time Will Be . . .

Another quality of voice is resonance. Many of us have learned to speak in ways that decrease the impact of our com-

munication. Some speak through the nose, giving the voice a nasal, whining quality that is very difficult to listen to. Others slur words or mumble, making listening and understanding an effort. I have heard students speak from the back of their throat, giving the voice an extraterrestrial quality that might be okay for phoning another planet but will be a barrier to effective communication with kids. My high school speech teacher gave me some advice that was extremely helpful for overcoming a high-pitched, nasal-sounding voice.

First, always start with plenty of air. Words cannot be spoken with clarity, quality, or intensity without air. For example, try this exercise: Exhale, then say "wonderful." Next, take a deep breath, then say "wonderful." Hear how much clearer the word sounds when spoken with lungs full of air?

Breathe from your diaphragm, not just from your chest. Put your hand on your stomach just where your rib cage ends. Now take a deep breath. If your hand moves inward, you are breathing shallowly from the lungs. If your hand moves outward, you are breathing deeply, fully using your diaphragm. Breathe. It not only gives you life, it gives your speech life.

Second, always allow the words to reach the tip of your tongue before speaking them. Say the sentence in quotes below. Do not allow the words to reach the tip of your tongue, but force them out from the back of your throat. You will find it necessary to pinch the muscles in your throat a bit to keep the words back there. Ready? Now say, "Kids, I want you to know God loves you." Did you hear? You sounded like a Martian.

Now look around to make sure you haven't attracted a UFO full of aliens who think you're a lost member of their tribe. If none are present, repeat the same sentence. This time allow the words to reach the tip of your tongue. Be sure to open your mouth and let the words explode from the tip of your tongue past your teeth. Ready? Take a deep breath and say, "Kids, I want you to know God loves you." Did you hear how much clearer your pronunciation was? The words were much more crisp and interesting, and there was much less temptation to speak through your nose. Speak from the tip of your tongue.

Speed: Where Is the Fire?

When it comes to speed, speaking is like driving. Very few drivers are arrested for driving too slow, but each year thousands are caught driving too fast. Most errors in the speed of a speech are on the side of talking too fast. Although the human mind is capable of comprehending speech delivered at incredible rates of speed, this kind of comprehension is possible only if the listener is totally motivated and relaxed, with no distractions.

When speaking under usual circumstances, one's speech should be relaxed—conversational pace or slightly faster. Speaking too fast causes your audience to miss phrases and ideas. Most teenagers will quickly tire of trying to keep up. Fast talking also intimidates an audience. You have heard the phrase "fast-talking salesman." It is always used derisively. A deliberate, well-paced delivery conveys a sense of confidence and trust and will hold an audience's attention much more effectively.

Variety: The Spice of Life

In a television program centered around a small girl who was a robot, the importance of variety in speech was graphically demonstrated. The girl's role was limited because she had to speak in a monotone. All of her sentences were delivered in the same tone, at the same volume and pitch, and without facial expression. Television viewers never had a chance to like this little girl because she was a robot.

We have all fallen asleep during monotone, lackluster speeches. Don't be a robot. Vary your pitch to create drama, excitement, distress, or other emotions. Vary your volume. A shout to appropriately emphasize a point will bring back a wandering mind; a whisper at the right moment will keep the kids on the edge of their seats. Don't fall into the habit of droning through a Sunday morning lesson. If you do, your kids will form a habit of shutting you off before you even begin.

Listen to yourself on tape. Would you pay attention? Look at your audience. Are their eyes open? Are they looking at you or are they involved in a game of tic-tac-toe? Are they fascinated with a spider slowly making its way across the ceiling? Any of these symptoms will hint that you may be a boring speaker, and you may need to add variety to your voice. Variety is not only the spice of life, for the youth speaker it is life itself.

LANGUAGE: KEEP IT SHARP AND CLEAR

Often we are lazy in developing our ability to effectively use the English language. Many of us are deathly afraid of silence. The result is that when we lack something to say, we continue to talk using words that have absolutely no purpose other than to fill time.

The word "ah" is used prolifically by speakers trying to think of their next word. It's sad that we are unaware we are using these words. Many of my students will say the word "ah" twenty to thirty times in a five-minute talk—about once every ten seconds. Sometimes speakers will listen to themselves on tape and be amazed to hear themselves say "ah" four or five times in a row while gathering their thoughts. If you say "ah" twenty to thirty times during a five-minute talk, about one-tenth of your speech consists of a word that has absolutely no meaning.

Other filler words that have absolutely no meaning are *so, like, ya know, um, okay.* Avoid them! Silence is not an enemy. In fact, a moment of silence while you search for an appropriate word will add to the dynamics of your talk. Kids pick up bad habits of speech so fast that they spread like a disease throughout the culture. Presently the word "like" is used as every form of speech imaginable. Does this sound familiar? "I was *like* driving home from *like* school when I *like* came up to this *like* accident. It was *like* so gross." DO NOT! I repeat, DO NOT be deceived into believing that adopting this incoherency will make you more accepted as a speaker. Speak as an intelligent adult with purpose and clarity.

Good preparation will be your best friend in ridding your speeches of filler words. Record yourself practicing the speech you have prepared. Listen to the tape and note the places you groped for the right word. List the words and phrases you used to fill space. Find the right words to replace fillers and plan to use them. Tape yourself again and recount the number of filler words you use. Notice how your use of filler words drops dramatically. This is because you're aware of their use, you're consciously avoiding them, and you're prepared because you know what you're going to say.

> **For somebody felt something so much that he gave something so that somebody wouldn't have to experience something but could have something.**
> **John 3:16**

> **"Aren't you glad the Bible isn't full of filler words?"**

Next, search your speech for two other meaningless words: "things" and "stuff." These words almost always can be replaced with more descriptive words. A friend of mine had an English teacher who failed any written paper containing the word "things." She said, "If you say 'The mountain was covered with trees and things,' I want to know what the 'things' are before I will go on the mountain." If the mountains are covered with trees and rocks, then knowing the things are rocks makes the speech more picturesque and interesting. If the mountains are covered with trees and giant killer worms, then the speech is very interesting indeed, and the teacher will probably stay home and not go to the mountains!

You can be a much more effective communicator by following the "stuff" above. See what I mean? What stuff? Avoid meaningless words. Strive for an excellent command of the English language by saying what you mean: You can be more effective by following the advice given above.

PART THREE
PROGRESS:

Advanced 💋 Lip Moves

CHAPTER EIGHT

Verily, Verily, Thy Audience Sleepeth

It's been proven that humor heals, breaks down barriers, and is a tremendous asset to basic communication. You don't have to be a comedian to develop and use humor. It's also been proven that opening the covers of the Bible can cause one to feel drowsy. This need not be. So smile, and let's learn together how to brighten our teaching of Scripture.

USING HUMOR: WHAT'S SO FUNNY ABOUT THAT?

Of all the sections in this book, this is my favorite. I have spent the last twenty-five years making my living using humor. Humor has given me the tremendous privilege of ministering to thousands of kids and adults throughout the world. I believe that nothing softens hard hearts, breaks down walls of cynicism, and opens doors for crystal-clear communication like effectively used humor. Laughter is a therapeutic exercise that clears the head and heart. Used in a speech, it gets the blood flowing and creates great interest. Humor requires a common point of understanding that builds almost instant rapport with an audience. Jokes and humorous anecdotes are structured to ensure that everyone starts from the same point of understanding. A simple humorous story can accomplish what a whole speech couldn't.

Humor also provides speakers with instant feedback. Speakers who do not use humor have only subtle cues by which they can judge their success: Has anyone left? Are those that remain throwing anything? A speaker may assume that listeners who look directly at him or her are hanging on every word. In reality, these listeners may be reliving a date, grappling with a problem at home, or lying on a sun-drenched beach a thousand miles away. The speaker has no way of knowing if the kids are really listening. If, however, the speaker uses a humorous story to illustrate a point and the audience responds in laughter, then the speaker knows there has been a bond of interest and understanding.

The terrifying aspect about humor is that when the response to an attempt at humor is met with silence and blank stares, it can kill what started to be a good speech. It also can kill the communicator if he or she has a weak heart. That's why when comedians get no laughter, they say they died onstage. Failing at humor is just like dying . . . only worse. At least when you die in life there is the chance of going to heaven. Let's go through some steps to develop humor in your communication.

Be Natural

As we discussed in a previous chapter, it is essential that you be yourself. Let the humor of your speech show through your personality. If you are usually serious, you will probably be more comfortable with dry, witty humor. Most likely, neither Mark Twain nor Will Rogers would have lasted very long as stand-up comedians, but their satire and wit are marks of their ability as communicators. They were humorists.

Having a sense of humor is not synonymous with being a comedian. An intellectual, witty style of subtle humor often lends itself more effectively to good communication than it does to outright comedy. Comedy lends itself more to entertainment and, as such, can be used as an excellent tool to open minds for communication. I have taught the use of humor in communication for years. I find that it's much easier to help a good communicator develop a sense of humor than it is to help a good comedian learn to use comedy to communicate.

Far too often after the first few disastrous attempts at humor, a speaker will give up. Those of us who have experienced the pain of failure can understand why. However, we often fail because of the way we try to introduce humor into our talks. Many speakers set themselves up for failure by attempting a high-risk kind of humor.

> Yesterday, my daughter said something hilarious [this setup demands laughter]. We were playing a Bible trivia game. The question I asked her was, "Why did God expel Adam and Eve from the Garden of Eden?" She thought for a moment, then responded, "Because they ate the Fruit of the Loom."

If no one laughs, you're in serious trouble. Because of the way you set yourself up, people must laugh or you've obviously failed. Unless you're absolutely sure of yourself, never set up a humorous story by saying "I heard a great joke today" or "You're going to love this one" or "My daughter said something hilarious." If people don't think it's a great joke or if they don't love it, you're dead! And as you probably already know, once you're dead, communication is very difficult!

The previous story could be presented in a low-risk way. Assume your objective is to demonstrate the importance of obedience to God's commands. Then you can use the story to set up a talk about Adam and Eve's sin. You could present the story as follows:

> Last night I was playing a Bible trivia game with my daughters. I asked my daughter Taryn, "Why did God expel Adam and Eve from the Garden of Eden?" After a moment of thought, she responded, "Because they ate the Fruit of the Loom." My daughter may have misunderstood the menu, but she identified the problem: disobedience.

Now if there is laughter, enjoy it; if not, you're still alive. You can continue. "Our whole family laughed at her answer. But in a way, her answer didn't matter. It didn't matter if Adam and Eve ate the Fruit of the Loom, an apple, a watermelon, or the tree itself. The point is, they disobeyed." Use the humorous story to illustrate a point rather than just to entertain. Then whether the audience laughs or not, the story served a purpose. You won't be embarrassed if the audience doesn't laugh, because you didn't tell them to expect to laugh. If they don't laugh, you'll have a chance to tell the story again a bit differently to another group. You may then discover the timing and wording that will make it funny. If they do laugh, wow! What a bonus. Either way, you get your point across.

I'm willing to use high-risk humor with the following story. While my family and I were camping in the wilderness recently, we found we were unable to attend church. My oldest daughter, Traci, volunteered to preach a sermon, so we held an impromptu wilderness service. Part of her sermon was to question the family on our Bible knowledge. It took me fifteen minutes to regain my composure and stop rolling down the mountain after my youngest daughter, Taryn, answered the question, "How did God create people?"

Without hesitation and with the enthusiasm that only a child can express, Taryn answered, "First God made man. Then he noticed man was lonesome. So he put him to sleep, took his lungs out, and gave them to some woman."

Never Allow Humor to Cloud the Message

Humor is a powerful tool to enhance communication, yet when misused it can destroy communication. Humor that is in bad taste can negate anything good you will say. Contrary to popular belief, kids are not enamored with gross or cruel humor *unless* they are conditioned by their leaders to accept that kind of humor. What is acceptable for one audience may not be acceptable to the next. These are judgment calls you must make carefully. Set your standards high. A truly good comedian can be funny in good taste. Strive for the best in this area.

Sometimes humor can be used as a weapon to hurt people; other times, it can hurt unintentionally. We live in a culture where being teased is a sign of acceptance. There are those who would say that this kind of good-natured ribbing should not be practiced among Christians. I disagree. I believe one of the values of humor is that it gives humans a painless way of saying that we recognize each other's weaknesses and accept each other in spite of them. Yet, the same teenage culture that uses teasing and humor as tools of social acceptance also uses humor as a weapon to hurt those of whom they disapprove. We never should allow our humor to slip into that category.

I once shared the platform with Alvin Law, a young Canadian communicator who was born without arms. We were fielding questions from an audience of approximately 2,000 teenagers. They would ask a question and one of us would answer. I had answered three consecutive questions when a boy stepped to the microphone and asked, "What is it like to go through life without arms?" The audience was dead silent at this direct question.

After a moment of uncomfortable tension, Alvin stepped to the microphone, winked at me, and said, "Ken, I'd like to answer this one." The tension was immediately dissolved as we laughed and realized there was no reason to be tense. It is important to know that only Alvin could deliver that line. If I had said, "Alvin, I think that question is for you," Alvin may have thought it was funny because he is my friend. But hundreds of students who didn't know of our friendship could have thought I was being cruel. Humor is like a double-edged sword. Be sure you know which edge the audience will feel.

One final caution: The audience's positive reaction to humor is a heady experience. It is easy to fall back on just being funny at the expense of not communicating. We must never forget that our message of Christ's love is of utmost importance. Humor is simply a powerful tool that dramatically opens doors for us to communicate that message.

Look for Humorous Stories in the World Around You

God has given us so much to observe and use in a humorous way to enhance our communication. Very humorous routines and poignant lessons can be drawn from some simple concepts. Here are a few examples:

Bill Cosby is one of the most successful comedians ever. He draws almost all of his material from the experiences of everyday life. He developed a routine around the way a dog greets his master with unrestricted joy; he developed another hilarious routine around the fear of going to the dentist; and he developed hours of material around the family communication theme.

Humor can make the audience sensitive and receptive to serious points. Richard Pryor, in spite of his excessive use of vulgar language, can bring one to tears of laughter and sorrow when he recalls his cocaine addiction. I watched in amazement as he used humor to drive home the tremendous impact his trip to Africa had on his life. Jerry Seinfeld has made millions showing us the humor in the minute and mundane details of everyday life. I built a comedy routine around a collection of over 200 barf bags (the ones airlines provide) I've accumulated from all over the world.

Know What Makes an Idea Funny

The three main elements of humor are surprise, exaggeration, and truth. Any humorous story or joke can contain any one or a combination of these elements.

Many jokes use surprise as the key factor. The story leads to a logical conclusion and the punch line takes you in another direction.

"Did you hear the one about the guy who fell out of an airplane?"

"Oh, that's bad."

"No, that's good. He was wearing a parachute."

"Oh, that's good."

"No, that's bad. It didn't open."

"Oh, that's bad."

"No, that's good. There was a haystack beneath him."

"Oh, that's good."

"No, that's bad. There was a pitchfork sticking up in the haystack."

"Oh, that's bad."

"No, that's good. He missed the pitchfork."

"Oh, that's good."

"No, that's bad. He missed the haystack."

The length of this joke leads one to believe there is going to be a miraculous rescue, but the final line leaves you surprised at the abrupt end of the joke—not to mention the abrupt end of the poor guy's life. When my daughter answered the trivia question with "God chased Adam and Eve out of the Garden because they ate the Fruit of the Loom," it was the surprise of her play on words that caused us to laugh. Humor that uses surprise as its element is high-risk and the most difficult kind of humor to do well.

Other humor depends on exaggeration. Last night I listened to a comedian explain the trouble he has with his dog. He named his dog "Stay." His dog gets so confused when he calls him: "Come, Stay! Come, Stay! Come!" As I pictured this exaggerated scene, I began laughing and didn't stop until I was on the floor!

Exposing simple truth often brings laughter. When someone helps us see the truth that we have ignored, we are often able to laugh at ourselves. In one of my routines, I point out that parents say things that don't make sense. Only parents will yell out the back door, "If you cut your legs off with that lawn mower, don't come running to me!" Only parents will ask a child questions they don't want the child to answer; for example, "Do you think I'm stupid?"

Sometimes we laugh when we're forced to recognize the simple, silly truth. Sometimes that truth isn't really so silly. A mother spent half of a plane flight trying to settle down her young daughter. The little girl was bothering other passengers and running in the aisles. Several times the harried mom had set the daughter firmly in her seat only to see her squirt away at the first opportunity. Finally, in exasperation, the mother

plopped the girl in her seat and fastened her safety belt tightly about her. "Now sit still," she said firmly. A smirk spread across the girl's lips as she sat quietly for several minutes. "Why are you smiling?" the mother demanded.

"Because," replied the little girl, "I may be sitting on the outside, but I'm still jumping around on the inside."

The truth is funny and tragic. How many teenagers do you know who are peaceful on the outside but going wild on the inside? The previous story is a great example of low-risk humor. When I tell this story, people usually laugh. But even if they didn't, what an illustration!

The next time you hear a funny story, first enjoy it. But later ask yourself, "What made me laugh?" If you can identify what makes an idea funny, then you can make an idea funny yourself.

While doing a comedy concert in a large church in Texas, I was interrupted as paramedics removed a man from the audience. This kind of interruption has a way of putting a damper on comedy. We finished quickly and ended the concert. Later, I discovered that the man had been removed because of a heart attack. Since this attack had occurred while people were laughing hysterically, I felt somewhat responsible and wrote the man a letter of apology. I'll treasure his return letter above all the reviews and accolades I have ever received. He said, "Ken, I don't worry about dying. I prepared to meet my Lord many years ago. And please don't feel bad about the heart attack. I've had four heart attacks. I want to thank you for the best heart attack I ever had. I'll recover to laugh again. Keep bringing Christ's joy to others."

This man knows the real source of joy. His letter reminded me of the value of humor and I won't forget it.

BRINGING LIFE TO THE TEACHING OF SCRIPTURE: WHO KILLED THE BIBLE PEOPLE?

Next time you observe a speaker, watch for the following group reaction. The speaker is telling jokes, a story, or even delivering an interesting talk. He picks up a Bible or indicates in some way that he is going to quote from Scripture. In many audiences you will observe a change in attitude—a preparation for boredom.

Now consider this statement: I believe we have conditioned our young people to be bored with the Scripture. Over the years we have so mystified, spiritualized, and bled the Scripture of life that we have conditioned boredom. We can undo that conditioning. It took us hundreds of years to dare to translate the Gospel into modern-day language that is meaningful to the modern person. Many kids approach the Bible with the same relish they approach their studies of Shakespeare—a book of the past, for the past. Many of us, afraid that a modern translation might compromise the truth, stand our ground. "If the King James Version was good enough for the apostle Paul, it's good enough for me." Prior to the 1500s the Bible, written in the original Hebrew and Greek, was not available in languages common to the people. During that century several people tried translating the Scripture to English. In 1611 some wise "youth directors" persuaded King James that another attempt was needed to make the language understandable to the people of that period. Of course the more conservative pastors went ballistic. Following are two important ways to make the Scripture come alive for teenagers today.

Allow your kids to read the Bible in a language they speak— encourage them to read it often. Sometimes we underestimate our kids' intelligence as well as the Holy Spirit's ability to speak to them through the Scripture. If we pass on to the kids the idea that only seminary graduates are qualified to understand the Word of God, then I doubt we'll ever be able to interest them in the contents of the book. We are not asking young people to interpret the "correct" meaning of every passage; we are asking them to believe that God's Spirit will show them the truth and that the truth can change their lives.

Encourage kids to see the characters of the Bible as real—present the characters that way. These men and women did not walk around in Bible poses with halos hanging over their heads. They were human beings—with human feelings, emotions, and reactions. They felt anger and deep sorrow. They made mistakes. They fell in love and laughed together. The Scripture clearly shows that our Lord became a man and sacrificed his life for us. His deity is not threatened by his humanness.

Often we present Bible characters as sterile and unbelievable rather than as the humans they really were. These people didn't observe Christ's miracles with bored spiritual mutterings. There must have been times when their eyes almost popped out of their heads. When Peter spotted Jesus walking on the water, I doubt if he yawned, "Verily, someone walketh on the water." I'll bet the boat almost tipped over as everyone crowded to one side to see. Do you suppose Peter's heart rate was normal when he accepted Jesus' invitation to step out and join him? No way! If Jesus were to walk on water today, the cameras would be clicking like crazy. The skeptical press might report the incident the next day: "Jesus can't swim."

Sometimes presenting Bible stories as they would have happened in a modern setting helps bring them to life. It also helps if we are excited about the Bible. For instance, have you ever thought of how desperately Zacchaeus wanted to see Jesus? He climbed a tree. Before you respond by saying, "So what? Bible people did that kind of thing all the time," think a moment. Zacchaeus was a hated tax collector who, I'm sure, wanted to keep a low profile. When was the last time you saw your IRS agent in a tree?

There were times when Bible people laughed together. Elton Trueblood wrote an excellent book titled *The Humor of Christ*. It should be required reading for any person who wishes to bring the delight of the Scripture to young people. Trueblood's book reminded me of a portion of Scripture that has always brought a smile to my face. In Matthew 19:24 Jesus said to his disciples, "It is easier for a camel to go through the eye of a needle than for a rich man to enter the kingdom of God." I get a mental picture of what I read. How could I get a camel

through the eye of a needle? Would I start with the tail? I'll tell you one thing, if I ever succeeded in threading a camel through a needle, he'd be one strung-out camel!

Instead of bringing this story to life, we kill it by discussing whether the camel was a real camel or a rope, or whether the eye of a needle was a needle's eye or a hole in a city wall called "the eye of the needle." No wonder kids yawn when we open the Bible. The point of the camel illustration is that Jesus was suggesting a ridiculously impossible task. This is demonstrated by the disciples' response, "Who then can be saved?" However, Christ's love is greater than any impossibility. His love could even get through to a person who loved money. The Lord said, "With man this is impossible, but with God all things are possible." I love this story. I love its basic truth, and I still would like a snapshot of the camel right after he came through the needle.

There were times when the disciples must have wept together. If I saw someone who had been lame all his life, healed and dancing in the street, there would be tears all over the place. And think of the combination of terror, joy, and confusion when the disciples were greeted by their risen Christ— their dear beloved leader whom they were sure was dead.

The Bible is not dead, but we can make it seem dead in the eyes of our young people if we drain the life from it with a stodgy, unfeeling approach.

Avoid the Temptation to Spiritualize Everything

I believe in the inerrancy of Scripture and in its divine inspiration. However, I'm aghast at the efforts we'll sometimes expend to draw some great spiritual lesson from every word. I remember a particular Sunday school class that I attended with my cousin Jim. The teacher was discussing a Bible verse one phrase at a time and then asking members of the class to tell what they thought the phrase meant. The members of the class were parroting back to the teacher the kinds of answers she wanted to hear. Even at that young age, I couldn't believe what I was hearing.

One boy was asked to explain the phrase "and the disciples left the house." Dutifully, the boy thought for a moment and then in a quavering, religious voice, immortalized this bit of wisdom: "The four walls of the house represent four kinds of sin—the lust of the eyes, the lust of the flesh, the lust of money . . ." Here he paused. I could see he was running out of lusts. There were four walls; if this interpretation was going to be good, he had to come up with one more lust. ". . . and the lust of lying," he continued. "When they walked out of the house, they escaped from the clutches of those lusts and from the evil of Satan, represented by the roof."

I could see his self-delight with that last bit of divine improvisation. He was richly praised for his interpretation of this portion of Scripture. My cousin was bent almost double trying to keep from bursting out in laughter. Seeing him about ready to explode, the teacher scowled. "Perhaps you have a better interpretation, Jim."

His face became sober, but I could still see a smile tugging at the corners of his mouth. Adopting the proper quavering voice he said, "This is a verse that has touched my soul. When the Scripture [he even rolled his first *r* in *Scripture* the way some preachers do] says the disciples left the house, I believe that God is trying to tell us . . ." Here he paused, looking heavenward. "He's trying to tell us that the disciples left the house."

When the laughter died down and the teacher had wounded Jim with her righteous glare, the class continued. But Jim was right. It didn't take a degree in Greek to know that the words were simply communicating that the disciples left the house. Unfortunately, the kids in my Sunday school class were learning that the Bible was to be manipulated to say what we want it to say. Even at that age, many resented not only that approach but the Bible itself.

Instead of attempting to mold the Bible to say what we think it should say and make it fit our preconceived ideas, we

need to teach young people to read the Bible with an expectation that God's Spirit will direct them through his Word. If we really believe that God can change our lives, we can help the Bible come alive in kids' lives.

Provide Application of the Bible's Truth

The greatest way to help kids live out the commands and truths of the Bible is to give them practical applications for their own lives. Many committed teenagers search the Word for direction. When you discuss loving each other, suggest that the students begin by telling their parents they love them. Give them a practical and achievable way of applying what you have taught. When you teach about our responsibility to help those who are less fortunate, provide an opportunity for kids to repair a widow's home or visit an elderly neighbor. The experience will imprint the lesson in their minds more deeply than all the fancy words you could ever say. Of all the secrets of bringing the Bible to life, this one is most important: Scripture is most real and alive when it is applied.

CHAPTER NINE

Special Applications

Throughout your ministry you probably will encounter situations that require a change in approach, such as speaking to the same audience, speaking to a small group, or speaking to different age-groups. Following are some special applications to help you adapt to these situations.

SPEAKING TO THE SAME AUDIENCE: HAVEN'T I SEEN YOU BEFORE?

This section is designed for people who speak to the same audience week after week. Many times one looks in admiration at the "hired gun" communicators who travel from place to place "wowing" every audience with their great deliveries. Please understand that these speakers have a pocketful of tried-and-proven messages. Many times these messages are given over and over again. All of the kinks have long ago been worked out. The funny parts are surefire, and practice has made the talks close to perfect. As one of those hired guns, I can tell you this, if you were to take any one of us and stick us in the same place for more than ninety days, requiring us to talk to the same audience two to three times a week, the candy-stick messages would soon be used up. To keep going, we would need some creativity, a commitment to the principles of this book, and dedication to the message of Christ's love.

The men and women who have gained my highest admiration speak regularly and successfully to the same group. Following are some keys to success for you.

Avoid the "Star Syndrome"

Oftentimes youth ministers become discouraged during their first few months of tenure. Many leaders are discouraged as a result of the "star syndrome." Those with the star syndrome define success as being regarded as the best by their peers in the ministry. They must be the star. Like the running back on a football team, it is only when they have the ball and are making a great play that they feel real fulfillment. Discouragement sets in when the youth group grows familiar enough to no longer be awed by their leader's presence. The pain is compounded when, around the same time, the leaders have used up all the plays in their playbook—all the best jokes have been told, and all the good meeting ideas have been used. The question looms: "WHERE DO I GO FROM HERE?"

The star syndrome is a serious threat to any youth leader's future, but it can be averted. Rather than feeling pressure to be a star each week, a healthier perspective is to think of yourself as a combination coach/quarterback. What a relief if you're not the one who always has to make the winning plays. Instead, use every resource available to help you achieve the objectives of your teaching. One week, hand off the ball to a film and allow it to carry the weight of communication. Another week, hand off the ball to a guest speaker. Other members of your team that can relieve pressure are short stories, music, videos, role plays, informal discussions, audiotapes, Bible studies, student-led meetings, and sometimes, for a break, fun nights out. Some groups have great success allowing the kids to plan and execute meetings. Once they have faced the pressure of making a meeting work, they may even be more sympathetic and attentive when you do the meeting.

If you depend only on your lectures as teaching tools, you'll quickly become a burned-out star. Experiential learning

can give the star some relief. Studies have shown that people learn best when they are involved. You can give an outstanding speech on "understanding parents," but a role play forcing the students to look at a situation from the parents' point of view will bring understanding that your speech never could.

I remember a man who spoke on priorities. The speaker not only talked to us, he involved us in his speech. He had us write on five pieces of paper the five most important things in our lives. He then made us prioritize our choices by burning each piece of paper, one at a time, until we had only one left. To this day I can remember what was written on that final piece of paper. I was forced to decide what one aspect was most important to me at that time in my life.

I will forever be indebted to Mrs. Peterson, a speech teacher, who instead of just teaching the principles of good speech, made me speak. That bit of experiential learning changed the whole course of my life. Use your creative ability to think of ways to involve your kids in learning. Experiential learning enhances your efforts at verbal communication. It is difficult for someone who likes to be in the spotlight to use some of these techniques. However, your survival depends on it. The star syndrome will either lead you to the frustrating end of your ministry or it will find you playing the starring role in many different churches for very short periods of time. If you find yourself riding this treadmill, get counsel and retrench. Be honest with your group and your supervisors, and then begin to share the load and the glory. The effort will be difficult but well rewarded by a more consistent ministry.

Avoid Being a "Bigger-and-Better Go-Getter"

Leaders with this malady expect to score a touchdown every play. This expectation is closely related to the star syndrome; it comes from a desire to be successful and drives the youth worker to try to have a bigger-and-better meeting every time. Once again, it's easier to prevent the pain that comes with this impossible expectation than it is to correct the problem once it has started. The secret is to always hold some troops in reserve. If you haven't already used all your best ideas, wait. Establish a pattern that provides your kids with the variations of communication previously mentioned (films, videos, guest speakers, and so forth). Each week the kids know the meeting will be stimulating, informative, and somehow different. Then, every once in a while, bring the reserves off the bench and run the full hundred yards for a touchdown. If you have established in your own mind that every play need not be a touchdown, and if you have committed yourself to making even the nonglamorous meetings quality efforts with a specific objective, then you won't end up feeling guilty or trying to make each meeting top the preceding one. Your students will come to expect quality at every meeting and look forward to a crowd-pleasing touchdown on special occasions.

Coaching Beats Playing

Realize that your long-term success is determined more by your work on the sidelines than by your spectacular plays as a speaker in front of the group. The more you get involved on an informal and personal level with your kids and the more available you are to them in their daily lives, the more they will respect you and listen to you when you are speaking up front. The kid who knows that you care about him because you visited his home this week will hear every word of your speech. Personal involvement with individual kids in your group will take you miles farther in ministry results than all the flashy eloquence and touchdown programming in the world. One of the keys is to keep your mind on the goal. Our goal is not to win an Oscar for best programming or greatest orator (although we may strive for excellence in both of these areas). Our goal remains to tell the Good News of Christ and his love and to give our young people the inspiration and guidance to apply those truths to their lives.

All of the previous suggestions can only be implemented if you know the secret of long-range planning. If you wait until

the last minute to plan for the week, you'll never get out of the rut. However, if you expend the time and effort to plan ahead, you can give yourself a break. Long-range planning not only leads to better communication, it leads to longevity for youth communicators.

One final suggestion: Refresh your playbook at least once a year. Take advantage of one of the youth resource conferences throughout the country. Organizations like Youth Specialties, *Group* magazine, and National Network offer the latest in resources as well as great fellowship and networking with other youth workers from around the world. I believe that these conferences are invaluable for your own spiritual refreshment and encouragement. You will come home with your batteries charged and your playbook full of new ideas. Addresses and phone numbers of some of the best of these organizations are listed at the end of this chapter.

SPEAKING TO A SMALL GROUP: OKAY, FORM A CIRCLE . . . BOTH OF YOU

Most of the youth groups in this country are composed of less than twenty-five students. The rules of communication are as valid for these groups as they are for groups of one hundred or more. There are some special rules, however, that apply to a small group.

So often I have seen a teacher or youth sponsor stand in front of a small group and deliver a formal speech, week after week. Although there may be times when this approach will add special meaning and emphasis to the message, most of the time it is much better to speak informally to a smaller group. When I find myself in a group of less than ten participants, I almost always ask them to form a circle so everyone feels included. Even in groups of ten to twenty-five people, I ask them to pull in tightly to form a cozy unit. In this way, it is possible to establish an intimacy that would be impossible with more people.

Another strategy small group leaders can use is to plan to get together for occasional large gatherings such as Christian concerts, conventions, and festivals. Many times young people feel as though they are all alone in the faith. A trip to a Christian concert or large gathering can revitalize a small group. The event gives kids an insight into a large body of believers; they see that there are many young people who believe in Christ. Planning three or four activities like this a year generates enthusiasm and interest upon which you can build an effective ministry—no matter what the size of your group.

If I had to choose an audience for a comedy concert, I would choose a large group every time. However, if I had to communicate an important message from the heart, I would choose to speak to a small group. Small groups provide an intimacy that becomes fertile soil for learning. With a small group, interaction also can be used much more effectively. Questions and discussion lend credibility and deeper understanding to the subject. A small group takes away the pressure to perform. In fact, attempts to perform will probably be met with a less-than-enthusiastic response. The disadvantages of speaking to a small group are far outweighed by the advantages of intimately living with and loving the people to whom you minister.

To help make your presentations special, use all of the resources available to you. Movies, tapes, discussions, role plays, adult volunteers, and student leaders serve to bring variety and spice to your program and ward off the old "familiarity-breeds-contempt" syndrome.

Always program to make your input special. Avoid long announcements that tend to detract from the message you will present. Always keep your spoken message separate from the bureaucracy of announcements. Your students should know that when you speak, it's going to be short and interesting.

Prior to a talk, introduce yourself well. Avoid introducing yourself by saying, "Sit down and shut up! We're going to start the meeting now." Pause. Glare at the class. Then proceed.

Avoid beginning your meeting with boring announcements. "I want to remind those of you who are going on the ski trip that . . . blah, blah, blah." Sometimes we get so used to our audience that we take them for granted. Imagine the following scenario instead. Your audience has become used to short but excellent speeches from you. They also know that you do not speak every week. Last week they watched a film and discussed true commitment. This week's meeting began with one of the students leading the group in two songs. Another student had prepared a flip chart of upcoming events and gave the announcements. An adult volunteer prepared the participants for the lesson by leading them in a short prayer. At that point you stepped to the front and gave your message.

The best leaders of small groups always make the communication time excellent; they make extensive use of teenage leaders and volunteers. I am not suggesting you should never give announcements or be involved in some of the other aspects of leading a group; I am suggesting that you use the resources around you to create a sense of anticipation each time you speak and that you reward that anticipation with life, variety, and excellence.

Let me beat this drum one more time: So often we wait until the last minute to plan, then it's too late to book the film, prepare the materials for the group-involvement game, or contact the guest speaker from across town. So you stand up and give another last-minute, poorly prepared talk. (After all, it's such a small group!) If goals are set and plans are made well in advance, a world of options opens up that would never otherwise be available. If you give the kids your best, they will never know they are a small group.

Discussion questions, role plays, and other forms of group interaction are invaluable tools in helping you communicate effectively to a small group. Although these techniques are not the main subject of this book, a couple of observations can move you toward success in these areas.

Establish an Open Atmosphere That Encourages Discussion

Too many times discussion in a small group is more like a test. The leader asks a question, a few brave souls offer answers, then the leader gives the "right" answer. This kind of format leads to two negative results. The students either clam up for fear of giving the wrong answers, or certain students give the answers they think the leader wants to hear rather than what they really believe or feel.

Ask the kids to tell their feelings about a subject. Do not judge their answers or compare them with your opinions. If you ask their opinion, then respect their opinion and thank them for participating—even if you think their opinion is off base. When you give a talk and express your beliefs, you will expect the same kind of respect from the young people. Win the right to be heard.

A youth pastor once asked me to help with his group. The kids refused to take part in any kind of discussion. His group of about twenty kids exhibited all the buzzing and talking indicative of a live group of teenagers. They were polite and attentive during the first part of his talk. However, when he asked a question, he was answered by dead silence. The members of the group averted their eyes to avoid looking at him and possibly being called on. My presence made the situation even more awkward for the leader, so he pressed for someone to answer. Finally, to break the embarrassing silence, a boy volunteered his opinion. "You've got to be kidding," the leader sputtered, and then proceeded to cut the boy's opinion to shreds in front of everyone.

No wonder there was no discussion in this group! The leader didn't want discussion. He wanted the students to agree with whatever he said. Don't be threatened when a member of your group expresses an opinion that differs from yours. The exchange of ideas is fertile ground for learning. You may reply, "But we are trying to teach truth!" If the truth we are trying to teach cannot stand in the face of opposing ideas, then it must not be the same truth that Christ taught. Remember the boy who offered his thoughts and was shot down in front of everyone? How open do you think he is to the "truth"? If you won't listen to your kids' thoughts, how willing will they be to listen to yours?

The value of discussion is that it strengthens communication by allowing the open exchange of ideas. Your authority is not lost in this exercise. The strength of your message will not be lessened by unorthodox views that may be presented. On the contrary, because you respect the ideas of your group, they will listen more carefully to yours. You also will know where they truly stand on an issue. It is much better to have them disagree and express that disagreement than to have them hide their feelings and parrot what they think you want them to say. Like the Sunday school teacher who asked her students, "What has fur, a bushy tail, and collects nuts for the winter?" A little boy in the back hesitantly raised his hand. When the teacher called on him he said, "I think it's a squirrel, but I'm going to say it's Jesus." Remember, all good communication starts where the audience is. Discussion is a beautiful format for discovering exactly where they are.

Ask Questions That Require More Than a One-Word Answer

Instead of asking, "Susan, do you believe God really loves us?" ask, "Susan, why would anyone believe that God loves us?" In the first question she may answer yes or no, and the ball is back in your court. In the second question she is made to think. If ever a student questions the validity of a point in your message, break out the whistles and balloons and rejoice. You have just received clear evidence that you are a good communicator.

The same rejoicing would be in order when one of your kids can articulate one of your points well enough to demonstrate agreement. Far too often we think that the "good talk" compliment means we are doing well. Maybe the audience was simply entertained, or maybe the compliments are just a polite way to get out the door. But when we see evidence that our teenagers are thinking about, acting out, evaluating, and even questioning our propositions, it is at that point we know we are

doing our job well. Therein is the value of discussion and feedback—it is an excellent barometer of our progress.

You may have to train your kids to disagree respectfully. Do this by providing discussions where you challenge each other's ideas openly and courteously. Set the guidelines before the discussion. It is important at those times to be sure we are challenging and questioning the idea and not the person. "That's a stupid idea" is a challenge to my intellectual ability. "I disagree" is a challenge to my thought or proposition. "That's interesting, let me tell you what I think," is even more thoughtful. Establish an atmosphere where it is possible to disagree in love. This role is essential if you ever want kids from outside the group who are unfamiliar with your Christian concepts to feel comfortable. Always remember, a small group may not lend itself to big games or a "show biz" atmosphere, but a small group always lends itself to fantastic personal ministry and discussion.

SPEAKING TO DIFFERENT AGE-GROUPS: IDENTIFY AND ADAPT TO THE SUBDIVISIONS OF THE SPECIES

The principles we have discussed so far in this book are universal and necessary for effective communication to any audience. However, because we need to meet the listeners' needs, we must understand that each audience requires a slightly different approach in our method of speaking. In this section let's look at several age-groups and see what changes are necessary in our presentation to communicate effectively. The following is an overview, but it will give you an idea of the subtle changes necessary.

Adults

The people who make up this subspecies are unique because they almost always look as if they are listening. But don't be fooled. The only difference between adults and teenagers is that when teenagers get bored, they let you know it. Teenagers exhibit symptoms like rolling their eyeballs, yawning, and play-ing hidden games of tic-tac-toe. These symptoms sometimes degenerate to the dreaded activity of passing notes. Adults are more capable of absorbing content, but this should not be used as an excuse for not making the message interesting.

I just returned from a gathering of over 9,000 people where the youth were separated from the adults. After two days, the adults began to defect from the dry, tedious pro-gramming provided for them. They were coming to the youth programs by the hundreds. Why? Because being an adult is not synonymous with moving into the twilight zone of boredom. Adults need and want the same stimulating, interesting, and purposeful communication that teenagers demand. Adults are simply more tolerant and polite; they get bored peacefully. When adults are bored, they wouldn't consider throwing paper airplanes or thumping the person in front of them on the head; however, they may allow their heads to bob up and down and finally settle on their chests in a deep sleep. They can look right at you but actually be in Hawaii in their minds.

Adults do not appreciate insincerity or clowning around when it's out of place. They require a more sophisticated approach. But overall, the principles of good communication work with adults as well as with teenagers.

Junior High

Another interesting subdivision of the human species is the junior high age-group. Unlike adults, who can be looking at you and never hear a word you're saying, junior high kids can be climbing the walls and take to heart every word. Keep your message short, make it exciting, and say something that will count for eternity. They are listening, and they probably regard your word as gospel (all the more reason to be sure it is).

Junior high students are the most challenging audience of all. Ten years ago I stood in front of about 300 junior high stu-dents to speak. Sitting in the front row were two boys, exact-ly the same age. One was sitting with his arm around a girl.

He looked as if he had been shaving for a year. He was muscular, well-developed, and spoke with a deep, husky voice. He was physically involved with his girlfriend, and they were getting counseling from their youth director. Next to him sat the other boy, exactly the same age. He hated girls. His skinny little prepubescent body had never felt the sting of a razor. In a thin, reedy voice he would tell you that the closest relationships he had were with his parents, a friend named Ed, and a cocker spaniel.

What speech will meet the needs of both of these boys? One will listen to a talk about sex, the other will giggle. One will enjoy your opening skit, the other will think it's childish. Because of these differences, the two boys may not even want to be in the same group.

Outside of dividing into smaller groups, there is no way of solving this problem of diversity. Make the most of the situation by keeping all your programming exciting and short. My experience indicates that on a good day, about three to five minutes is the top attention span of a junior high student. If you are to keep the attention of this group, you must maintain an ever-changing, popping program. These kids can and do handle content, but it must be given in intense, short doses.

Before I proceed, you must understand that I avoided junior high audiences for many years. The reason was my misinterpretation of the way a junior high crowd responds. I found them to be a squirrelly audience who seemed to be living in a different world. They laughed in all the wrong places, they seemed not to listen for more than a few seconds at a time, and they squirmed constantly. I remember beginning one speech by saying, "Well, how's it going?" It was a rhetorical question; it wasn't meant to be answered. But about one hundred of these wriggling angels answered it simultaneously. Another fifty paid attention only when I mispronounced a word or made a slip of the tongue. At that time, they would verbally call the mistake to my attention. The timing to my comedy was ruined, and I didn't think they heard my message at all. I was wrong. Maybe junior highers wiggle because the adult butterfly is trying to escape from that child body. And maybe they don't respond like other humans, but they are listening. After the program, I discovered that they were unbelievably appreciative of the message.

Junior high kids possess a quality that will quickly disappear—a quality as precious as gold. They are moldable. Their hearts are open to change and, whether they show it or not, they usually are fiercely loyal to their leaders. The words you say go much deeper into their hearts than you'll ever know. If you don't believe that, think back to the influence of those who ministered to you when you were in junior high. The same words that can inspire them can be used to hurt and humiliate them. So handle with care.

High School

Although this entire book has been written for those who speak to high school age students, I want to suggest the following necessities for good communication with them. None of these are technical; they come more from the heart.

1. Practice what you preach. Teenagers will regard what you say with caution until they see it lived out in your life.

2. Don't be afraid to confront. Confrontation is part of any real love. Contrary to outward appearances, teenagers look for positive guidance given in a spirit of love. Guidelines provide a much needed sense of security and give direction to life. One look at the destructive result of an unguided, undisciplined child clearly demonstrates that fact. Sometimes, the truth hurts. But it is that same truth that sets us free.

3. Meet the kids in their world. If our communication with teenagers is to be meaningful and effective, we must meet them in their world. As youth workers, we are more aware than anyone that high school students are not breaking down the church doors to get to our

meetings. If we are to bring teenagers closer to Christ, we must meet them where they live. When Christ reached out to us, he didn't schedule a meeting in heaven and wait for us to show up. He came and lived among us. Nothing communicates our love to teenagers more than our willingness to go into their world to reach them. It is frightening and sometimes frustrating, but in the end, our words carry unbelievable power when backed by proof of our love.

RESOURCES

Youth Specialties
1224 Greenfield Dr.
El Cajon, CA 92021
619-440-2333

National Institute of Youth Ministries
Jim Burns
940 Calle Amanecer
#G
San Clemente, CA 92672
714-498-4418

Group Publishing
P.O. Box 481
Loveland, CO 80539
910-669-3836

National Network
Paul Fleischmann, Director
17150 Via Del Campo
San Diego, CA 92127
619-487-6900

CHAPTER TEN

A Final Challenge

Since writing this book, my speaking and my attitude toward communication have changed forever. Now that I have a standard by which to judge clarity and the tools to deliver messages with power, I cannot settle for mediocrity. The principles of SCORRE haunt me, continually driving me to a desire for growth and excellence in my communication. I hope this book haunts you as well. I hope these principles will take root like a seed—that once planted they will continue to grow throughout your life. I respect and admire those of you who have responded to the challenge of communicating the love of Christ to young people. Instead of the culmination of a lesson in communication, I hope this book is for you the beginning of a never-ending pursuit for excellence.

COMMITMENT TO GROWTH: KEEP ON KEEPIN' ON

I am saddened when I observe people who have ceased to grow. There have been times I could identify the year some people graduated from high school by the style of their hair—they have been frozen in time. They have refused to change and grow. There are countless numbers of entertainers who are no longer successful because they made great achievements and then relied on the glorious past to carry them into the future. Never stop growing in your communication skills.

For God so loved the world that he sent . . .

~~a special delivery letter~~

~~a singing telegram~~

~~a recorded cassette message~~

~~a videotape~~

HIS ONLY SON

The day you decide you are the best and stop striving to be better, you will place one foot firmly in a coffin, and your effectiveness will begin to die. The following are three ways you can continue to develop and excel as a communicator.

1. Continue the educational process. One is never too good to stop learning from seminars, books, educational classes, and other growth-stimulating resources. Whenever a new book on some aspect of communication comes out, read it. I firmly believe that reading is the very best activity that will make us better communicators. If a communication course is offered in your community, take it. Watch great communicators—not to steal their illustrations, but to see how they deliver those illustrations with excellence.

All the stolen illustrations in the world won't make you a better communicator, but knowing and applying the techniques used by great communicators will help you present any illustration in a more effective way. There is much to learn from watching others.

2. Establish a network of feedback. Although you'll be your own best critic, realistically you'll need a much more objective opinion. Your husband, wife, children, friends, even some of your youth can give you excellent feedback regarding your progress as a speaker. I usually ask someone at every speech to tell me where I was weak and how my speech could have been strengthened. I also ask them to point out any distractions I may have caused by my gestures, attitude, or delivery. Always ask these friends what they felt you were trying to accomplish with your speech. A relentless effort to know your objective and to impart that most-important truth to your audience with every talk will bring eternal results among the students to whom you minister. A side benefit for those who are in your feedback network is that they will by far be the best listeners in your group. Wouldn't it be wonderful if every member of your group were actively listening to hear what you were trying to say?

3. Whenever possible, audiotape your talks. You will see great improvement in your speaking by applying all of the suggestions in this book. But if I were required to give you only one tool to help you become a better communicator, I would give you a tape recorder. Nothing will make you work on the SCORRE method more than listening to yourself talk and not being able to figure out what you were trying to say. You will quickly decide to give your speech a thorough cleaning when you personally count thirty-five "ahs" or "ya knows" in your seven-minute speech. Taping your talks also gives you a realistic handle on your audience's reaction

to your humor. It takes discipline to tape every talk, and you'll quickly learn that you need not listen to the whole speech, but the effort will pay off a hundredfold. Videotape one of your talks at least once a quarter, then watch the entire tape. Video gives you a front-row seat to observe the nonverbal aspects of your communication. Get someone from your network to watch with you and encourage them to critique your presentation. Having their input will double the effectiveness of this exercise. If you wish to continue to grow as a youth speaker, tape your talks and then listen and watch. It's the best feedback you can get.

A SALUTE AND A PRAYER:
TO THE MEN AND WOMEN ON THE FRONT LINE

In many ways, my job as a comedian is so much easier than that of the youth worker. Traveling speakers have to develop only five or six talks (some have only one). Each time they appear, it is before a different audience. They get a chance to practice their illustrations over and over again. Except for rare occasions, there is no need for extensive preparation. And new ideas and material can be tested within the safe confines of a larger talk that the speaker already knows works.

On the other hand, the job of a youth pastor or Sunday school teacher entails speaking to the same audience. Once each week, and sometimes more, there is a necessity of preparing a new message. Instead of being introduced as a special speaker who just flew in from an engagement in Las Vegas, you are usually not introduced at all. The fanfare and excitement that accompany an outside speaker are not there.

Although these factors will cause you more work and demand an even higher degree of excellence from you as a communicator, in the long run, you have the advantage. You're not there just to entertain or to be an evangelistic "hired gun." You're there with those special young people week in and week out to administer the life-changing message of the Gospel.

When they hurt, you can cry with them; when they rejoice, you can celebrate with them. You have the tremendous opportunity to model in your life the message you communicate.

When I step on a stage in front of 1,000 teenagers and the spotlight comes on, the impact of my message can be diminished by all the flash. Kids tend to think, "Oh, if I could just be like him, then I could live like a Christian." They never get the chance to see me in real life. The very reasons that made the kids come have become a barrier that must be broken down through vulnerability and credibility on the stage. Many times I have left an auditorium hungry for the opportunity to live with a young person through the first weeks of his or her new commitment to Christ. There are times when I long for the personal contact you are privileged to have. No one calls my number with a problem. My house never gets "decorated" with toilet paper. These are badges of personal love that are proof that you live where the kids live, proof that you are Christ's messenger walking among them, proof that you will be there when your young people need you.

So when the glamour of the road begins to twinkle in your eye, be reminded that you are the one in a position to really change lives. As a youth worker you may not know how important you are as a role model. Interviews, counseling, and casual conversations reveal that you are idolized, looked up to, and watched constantly. For many of your kids, you are their only serious Christian role model.

A song contains these words: "We don't need another hero." I believe the words to this song are correct. However, our youth do need someone they can trust and respect who will point them to the greatest hero of all time—Jesus Christ. As a parent, I look to you for a tremendous boost in helping my children grow up committed to Christ and living the faith. Because of the influence you will have on my children, I pray that you'll commit yourself to excellence in all your communication, that you'll commit your life to patterning the very message you present.